English G 21

Klassenarbeitstrainer
für Schülerinnen und Schüler

mit Lösungen
Lerntipps
Kompetenztest

D4 Erweiterte Ausgabe

Cornelsen

Deine Audios findest du hier:

1. Gehe auf scook.de.
2. Gib den unten stehenden Zugangscode in die Box ein.
3. Hab viel Spaß mit den Audios.

Dein Zugangscode auf
www.scook.de | sj4nt-sacum

Vokabeltrainer-App
Verfügbar für: iOS, Android und Windows Phone

English G 21 • Band D 4 Erweiterte Ausgabe

Klassenarbeitstrainer mit Lösungen, Lerntipps und Kompetenztest

Konzeption
Dr. Ursula Mulla und Nogi Mulla, Germering

Erarbeitet von
Bärbel Schweitzer M.A., Staufen

In Zusammenarbeit mit der Englischredaktion
Dr. Christiane Kallenbach (Projektleitung)
Gwendolyn Düwel, Lorraine Poulter (verantwortliche Redakteurinnen)
Susanne Bennetreu, Stefanie Juhnke (Bildredaktion)
sowie Sarah Silver

Beratende Mitwirkung
Martina Schroeder, Stedtlingen

Tonaufnahmen
Clarity Studio Berlin (Track 1-13)
The Soundhouse Ltd, London (Track 14)

Illustrationen
Carlos Borell, Berlin (S.12 (u. Lösungsheft S.7); 24 oben re.)
Constanze Schargan, Berlin (S.11; 13; 24 oben li.; 28; 37; 40; 43; 47)

Bildquellen
Alamy, Abingdon (S. 4 Mitte: les polders; S. 34: Spencer Grant; S. 54: Kimball Hall; S. 61 oben: Mirrorpix/Trinity Mirror; S. 62 oben: Alex Segre; S. 64: Mirrorpix/Trinity Mirror); **Art Explosion** (S. 56); **Caro**, Berlin (S. 24 Bild E: Riedmiller); **Corbis**, Düsseldorf (S. 18 oben: Reuters/Shannon Stapleton, unten: Reuters/BRENDAN MCDERMID; S. 24 Bild A: Kevin Burke; S. 52 unten: Bob Krist; S. 60 li. unten: Thomas Schweizer); **Getty Images**, München (S. 51: Panoramic images (RF); S. 52 oben: Getty Images; S. 60 re. Mitte: Kaz Mori; S. 62 unten: Lester Lefkowitz); **Grand Canyon National Park** (S. 5: NPS Photo); iStock, Calgary (S. 4 2.v. li.: Marko Cadez; S. 8 Bild 2: Gina Smith; S. 20 Bild 1: Margot Petrowski, Bild 2: Hope Milam, Bild 3: nycshooter, Bild 4: lilly3, Bild 5: Alina555, Bild 6: quavondo; S. 23: wdstock; S. 24 Bild D: J Morgan; S. 26 Bild 3: gremlin; S. 27: tomograf; S. 29: Sophia Tsibikaki; S. 32: kickers; S. 41 2. v. re. unten: Jason Titzer, 2. v. re. oben: digitalskillet, re.: Izabela Habur, 2. v. li.: Demid Borodin; S. 42 2. v. oben: Jochen Hank; S. 48: Kim Gunkel); **Picture Desk**, London (S. 66 re. oben: The Kobal Collection/Warner Bros. Pictures, li. oben: The Kobal Collection/Illumination Entertainment, li. unten: The Kobal Collection/Olive Bridge Entertainment, re. unten: The Kobal Collection/Twentieth Century-Fox Film Corporation); **Shutterstock**, New York (S. 4 re: Manamana, 2. v. re: Stephen Coburn, li.: Samuel Acosta; S. 6: Anton Foltin; S. 8 Bild 1: auremar, Bild 3: AVAVA, Bild 4: Monkey Business Images, Bild 5: Dolly; S. 14 oben: Losevsky Pavel, unten: Darren Hubley; S. 16 Jose Gil; S. 24 Bild B: Andresr, Bild C: tororo reaction; S. 26 Bild 1: SergeyIT, Bild 2: DDCoral, Bild 4: forestpath, Bild 5: Eduard Titov; S. 41 li: auremar; S. 42 oben: Yuri Arcurs, Mitte: miskolin, 2. v. unten: SunnyS, unten: Ina Schoenrock; S. 45: Roger Jegg – Fotodesign – Jegg.de; S. 49: Larisa Lcfitskaya; S. 50: Khirman Vladimir; S. 58: Monkey Business Images; S. 60 li. Mitte: Ivanova Inga, re. unten: mangostock, oben: Monkey Business Images; S. 61 re. unten: wavebreakmedia ltd, li. unten: Voronin76, Mitte: Monkey Business Images)

Textquellen
S. 5 *Become a Junior Ranger!* adapted from "Be a Junior Ranger" (http://www.nps.gov/grca/forkids/beajuniorranger.htm) (05.01.2011), © Grand Canyon National Park; S. 21 *The Empire State Building* adapted and abridged from http://www.esbnyc.com/observatory.asp (05.01.2011), © Empire State Building Company L.L.C.

Titelbild
Constanze Schargan, Berlin; Corel Library (US Flag Hintergrund)

Layout und technische Umsetzung
Heike Freund, Hameln

Umschlaggestaltung
Klein und Halm Grafikdesign, Berlin

www.cornelsen.de
www.EnglishG.de

1. Auflage, 6. Druck 2020

© 2011 Cornelsen Verlag, Berlin
© 2018 Cornelsen Verlag GmbH, Berlin

Das Werk und seine Teile sind urheberrechtlich geschützt. Jede Nutzung in anderen als den gesetzlich zugelassenen Fällen bedarf der vorherigen schriftlichen Einwilligung des Verlages.
Hinweis zu §§ 60 a, 60 b UrhG: Weder das Werk noch seine Teile dürfen ohne eine solche Einwilligung an Schulen oder in Unterrichts- und Lehrmedien (§ 60 b Abs. 3 UrhG) vervielfältigt, insbesondere kopiert oder eingescannt, verbreitet oder in ein Netzwerk eingestellt oder sonst öffentlich zugänglich gemacht oder wiedergegeben werden.
Dies gilt auch für Intranets von Schulen.

Druck: H. Heenemann, Berlin

ISBN 978-3-06-032253-4

PEFC zertifiziert
Dieses Produkt stammt aus nachhaltig bewirtschafteten Wäldern und kontrollierten Quellen.
www.pefc.de

INHALT

Unit			Seite
Introduction		Klassenarbeit	5
Unit 1	Klassenarbeit A	Reading • Language • Study Skills • Writing	11
	Klassenarbeit B	Listening • Language • Writing	16
Unit 2	Klassenarbeit A	Reading • Language • Mediation • Speaking	24
	Klassenarbeit B	Listening • Language • Mediation • Speaking	32
Unit 3	Klassenarbeit A	Reading • Language • Writing	37
	Klassenarbeit B	Listening • Language • Mediation • Speaking	45
Unit 4	Klassenarbeit A	Reading • Language • Writing • Speaking • Mediation	51
	Klassenarbeit B	Listening • Language • Mediation	56
Kompetenztest		Reading • Language • Writing • Speaking	61
Zusatz	Exam Skills	Listening • Speaking • Mediation • Reading • Words • Writing	67
		How to do well in a test	

ACHTUNG, KLASSENARBEIT!

Liebe Schülerin, lieber Schüler,
wer sich gut vorbereitet, kann der nächsten Klassenarbeit gelassen entgegen blicken. Der Klassenarbeitstrainer unterstützt dich ganz gezielt beim Üben für alle Klassenarbeiten. Du findest zu jeder Unit zwei Klassenarbeiten, mit denen du alle Fertigkeiten (skills) trainieren kannst, die du für die Klassenarbeiten benötigst.

Einige Tipps für ein erfolgreiches Lernen mit deinem Klassenarbeitstrainer:

Vorbereitung
Informiere dich genau über die kommende Klassenarbeit, damit du weißt, was dran kommt. In einem Lernplan legst du fest, welche Aufgaben du an welchem Tag bearbeiten willst. Plane dazu genügend Zeit ein. Hole dir bei Unklarheiten Hilfe. Am Tag vor der Arbeit wiederholst du nur kurz.

Lernheft
Führe ein Schreibheft für die Schreibaufgaben und zusätzlichen Übungen. Achte auf Übersichtlichkeit (Datum, Überschrift, Aufgabe, Seite). Lege auf der 1. Seite ein Inhaltsverzeichnis an. So kannst du bei Unklarheiten immer wieder nachschlagen. Es hilft dir auch, wenn du eine Aufgabe wiederholen möchtest.

Lösungsheft und Punkteschlüssel
Vergleiche deine Lösungen mit den möglichen Lösungen. Sieh dir dabei deine Fehler ganz genau an und überlege, was du falsch gemacht hast. Nur so kannst du daraus lernen und die Fehler in Zukunft vermeiden.
Im Lösungsheft findest du auch die Hörtexte und Lerntipps mit Verweisen zu weiteren Übungen.
Der Punkteschlüssel hilft dir, deine Leistung einzuschätzen.

Kompetenztest
Am Ende des Heftes findest du einen Kompetenztest, mit dem du dich auf eine zentrale Leistungsüberprüfung (auch: „Vergleichsarbeit", „Vera 8", „Diagnosearbeit", „Lernstandserhebung") vorbereiten kannst. Dieser Kompetenztest steht nicht in Zusammenhang mit einer bestimmten Unit im Buch.

Übrigens: Die Klassenarbeiten in diesem Heft prüfen das Gelernte sehr ausführlich ab. Du brauchst daher für die Bearbeitung länger als eine Schulstunde. Natürlich kannst du dir die Klassenarbeiten auch auf einzelne Tage aufteilen oder bestimmte Aufgaben ganz gezielt üben.

Let's get started!

Ich wünsche dir viel Freude und vor allem viel Erfolg beim Üben und Lernen mit deinem Klassenarbeitstrainer.

Have fun with English!

Bärbel Schweitzer

Introduction

READING

Become a Junior Ranger![1]

What is a Junior Ranger?

Junior Rangers are good friends of the Grand Canyon National Park. They learn about the Grand Canyon, have fun and represent the Grand Canyon to their friends, families and school back home. Junior Rangers know a lot about the park, so they can give information about it to others. They also help to protect the park and make sure that it stays as wonderful as it is today.

How can you become a Junior Ranger?

At the Grand Canyon, there are different ways to become a Junior Ranger. All of our Junior Ranger programs are free.

To become a Junior Ranger, pick up the Junior Ranger Activity Magazine at the Visitor Center at the Grand Canyon View Information Plaza. You must then do the activities you find in the magazine for your age group. There are different activities: for example you have to write about the park and answer questions on it, write poems and visit one of the Rangers' daily programs.

There are three different types of Junior Rangers for children ages 4+:

Ages 4–7: Raven

Ages 8–10: Coyote

Ages 11+: Scorpion

When you finish your activities, bring the magazine back to the Visitor Center and show it to a Ranger. Each Junior Ranger gets a Grand Canyon Junior Ranger certificate[2] and patch[3].

Phantom Rattler Junior Ranger (ages 4–14)

This is a very special program because only kids who hike or ride the mules down to the bottom of the Grand Canyon to Phantom Ranch can become Phantom Rattler Junior Rangers! There are two jobs you must do to become a Phantom Rattler Junior Ranger: first, you have to make it to Phantom Ranch, and second, you have to do the activities in the Junior Ranger magazine. If you do both, you will get your patch, a certificate and a baseball cap from a Ranger at Phantom Ranch.

---

[1] Junior Ranger ['dʒuːnɪə(r) 'reɪndʒə(r)] *jugendlicher „Park Ranger"*   [2] certificate [sə'tɪfɪkət] *Urkunde*   [3] patch [pætʃ] *Aufnäher, Abzeichen (aus Stoff)*

Introduction

1 About the text

Read the text. What are the two main ideas in the text? Write them down.

____ / 2

_____

_____

2 Junior Rangers and the Grand Canyon

____ / 8

Tick (✔) the correct box.

	Right	Wrong	Not in the text
1 Junior Rangers learn about the Grand Canyon.			
2 Children have to pay to go on a Junior Ranger programme.			
3 The Rangers' programmes take place once a week.			
4 Junior Rangers must be at least 4 years old.			
5 If you are 6 years old, you can become a Raven Junior Ranger.			
6 Junior Rangers can visit the Grand Canyon for free.			
7 Every Junior Ranger gets a baseball cap.			
8 Phantom Ranch is open 365 days a year.			

LANGUAGE

___/30

1 WORDS An alphabetical list

a) *The letters of the new words are mixed up. Put them in the correct order and write the words into the list. (7P)*

___/10

A	raeeudntv	N	eaivtN nrmAacie
B		O	
C	mteomcn	P	orlpte osnttia
D	iaydl	Q	
E		R	
F	ieogfvr	S	lsea
G	erdga	T	olto
H	whghyai	U	
I		V	
J		W	gnwi
K		X	
L	eesnlci ealtp	Y	
M	uoemmnnt	Z	eonz

b) *Write down six more new words that you have learned in the Introduction. (3P)*

2 Getting by in English

Write what you would say in English.

___/4

Was sagst du, …

1 wenn du sagen willst, dass du keine Ahnung hast, wohin du gehen solltest?

2 wenn du fragen willst, wie du zum Bahnhof kommst?

3 wenn du sagen willst, dass du keine Ahnung hast, was du machen sollst?

4 wenn du sagen willst, dass du keine Ahnung hast, wen du fragen könntest?

Introduction

3 GRAMMAR Talking about national parks

___ /6

*These people are talking about national parks. Complete the sentences. Use the **simple past** or the **present perfect**.*

1  I _____ (go) to the Grand Canyon with my family last summer.

2  I _____ (not hike) in the Grand Canyon yet.

3  Last week I _____ (give) a presentation on national parks in the US.

4  I _____ (not have) time yesterday to tell you about my trip to Death Valley.

5  We _____ (visit) many national parks in the past few years, but we _____ (not be) to the Grand Canyon yet.

👉 **Simple past** oder **present perfect**?

	Wann?	Signalwörter	Beispiel (positiv)	Beispiel (negativ)
Simple past	– Vergangenes – genauer Zeitpunkt	last weekend yesterday a week ago in 2007	I **went** to the Grand Canyon last weekend.	We **didn't go** to the Grand Canyon last weekend.
Present perfect	– Vergangenes – Zeitpunkt unwichtig	already, just, ever, never, yet	He **has** already **seen** a condor.	I **haven't seen** a condor yet.

4 GRAMMAR Junior Rangers on the internet

You want to know what it is like to be a Junior Ranger.
On the internet you find Andy Fischer's website. He's a Junior Ranger.

You decide to ask Andy some questions.
Complete the questions below in your exercise book.
*Use the **simple present** or the **simple past**.* (6P)

– what Park Ranger do to protect the park?
– why become Junior Ranger?
– programme with Park Ranger – interesting?
– how hear about Junior Ranger programme?
– what do to become Junior Ranger?
– where find out about Junior Ranger programme?

Fragebildung	
Simple present	**Simple past**
Are you a Junior Ranger?	Was it fun at the Grand Canyon?
Do you like the Grand Canyon?	Did you go to the Grand Canyon last weekend?
Does a Park Ranger know a lot about the park?	Did he become a Junior Ranger?

Now you

Write down four more questions you would like to ask Andy. (4P)

1 _____
2 _____
3 _____
4 _____

____/10

STUDY SKILLS

PARAPHRASING Andy explains

Andy explains some words to a German girl.
Can you complete his sentences?

1 A Park Ranger is _____
2 We sell baseball caps at the Grand Canyon. A baseball cap is _____
3 You can stay in a tent at the Grand Canyon. A tent is _____
4 There are bears at the Grand Canyon. A bear is _____

Paraphrasing

Zum Umschreiben kannst du oft Relativsätze verwenden.
Beginne deine Erklärungen dann so:

Bei Personen: A … is a person **who** …
Bei Gegenständen: A … is something **that** …
Bei Tieren: A … is an animal / a bird / a pet / … **that** …

____/4

Introduction

9

Introduction

WRITING   ____ /24

An article about the Grand Canyon

You want to write an article about the Grand Canyon for the school magazine.

a) Look at the mind map and complete it with your own ideas and the ideas from the box. (4P)

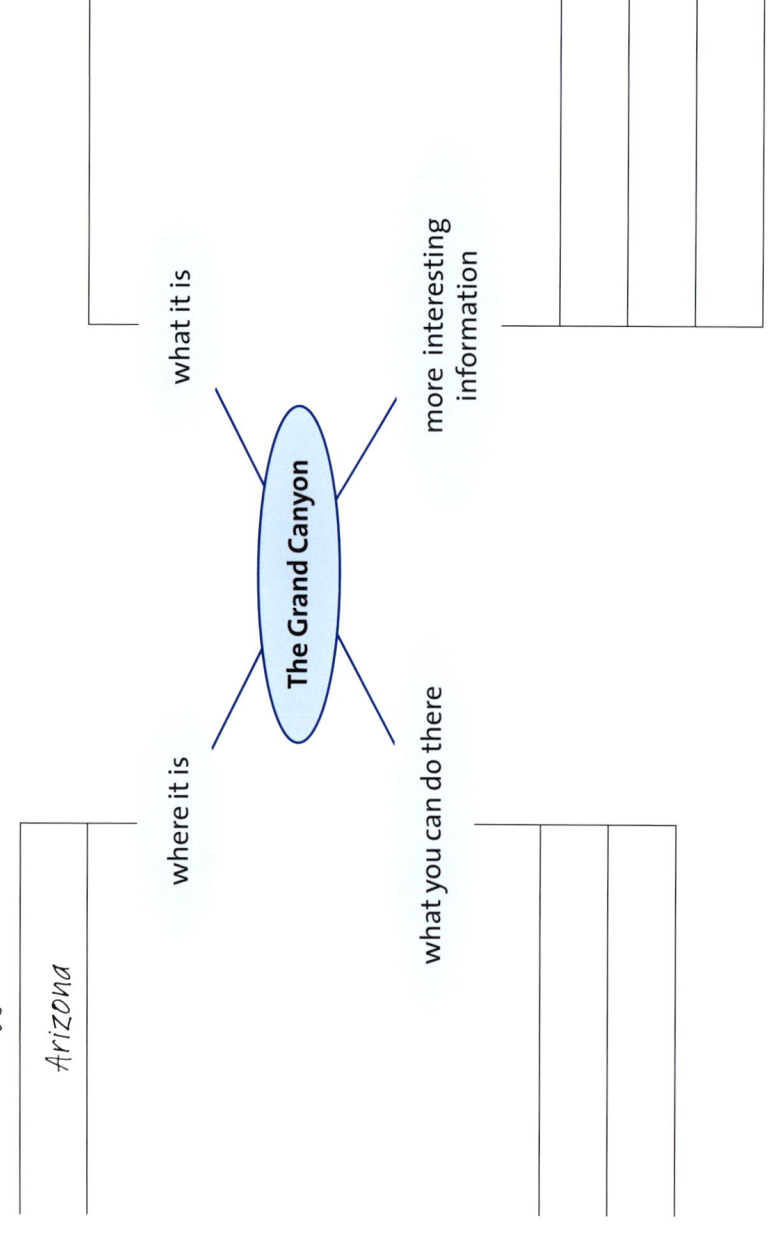

- bears
- go to rim and look across
- kids – Junior Rangers
- Park Rangers – protect park

- skywalk (good view)
- sleep in tents or motels
- walk into canyon
- walls of multi-coloured rocks

b) Write a text of about 100–120 words in your exercise book. (20P)

You can start your article like this:

About the Grand Canyon
The Grand Canyon is in the US, in the state of Arizona. It's ...

☞ **Texte schreiben**

Achte beim Schreiben darauf,
- ▪ deinen Text gut zu strukturieren. Die Mindmap gibt dir bereits eine Struktur für deinen Text vor.
- ▪ deine Sätze zu verbinden und auszubauen (z. B. linking words: **too, because, but, so, and**).
- ▪ ein passendes Ende für deinen Text zu finden.
- ▪ deinen Text inhaltlich und sprachlich zu überprüfen.

Klassenarbeit A

Unit 1

Gesamtpunktzahl ___ /60   Note ___

LISTENING

01 **Big Apple Radio**

You are on holiday in New York and are listening to Big Apple Radio.

☞ Versuche beim ersten Hören zunächst ganz allgemein zu verstehen, worum es in dieser Sendung geht. Vor dem Hören solltest du die erste Aufgabe lesen.

1 Subway stories

Listen to the radio programme. What are the people talking about? Tick (✔) the three correct pictures.
Be careful: there are three more pictures than you need.

___ /3

A

C

E

B

D

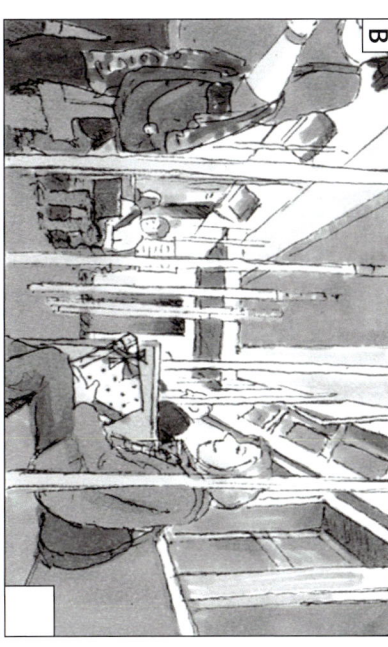
F

___ /12

11

Unit 1 | Klassenarbeit A

2 About the radio programme ___/9

Who is it? Read the sentences and tick (✓) the correct person.

	The presenter	Cindy	Sam	Ana-María
1 This person is talking about something that happened last spring.	☐	☐	☐	☐
2 This person is talking about something that happened last weekend.	☐	☐	☐	☐
3 This person was in a hurry.	☐		☐	☐
4 This person made a friend.	☐		☐	☐
5 This person has met lots of nice people on the subway.		☐	☐	☐
6 This person couldn't pay for his/her subway ticket.	☐	☐	☐	☐
7 This person works in the afternoon.	☐	☐	☐	☐
8 This person wants to say "thank you".	☐	☐	☐	☐
9 This person thinks that people in New York are friendly.	☐	☐	☐	☐

LANGUAGE ___/28

1 WORDS The five boroughs of New York ___/7

Write the names of the five New York boroughs onto the map. Then choose two boroughs and make notes about them.

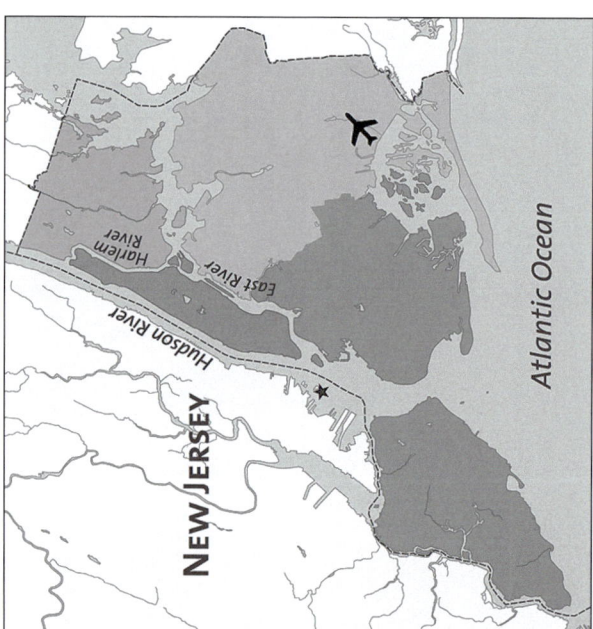

_____
_____
_____
_____
_____
_____

2 WORDS At the museum

Look at the pictures, then find the words and fill them in.
Be careful: with two words you have to find the correct form of the word.

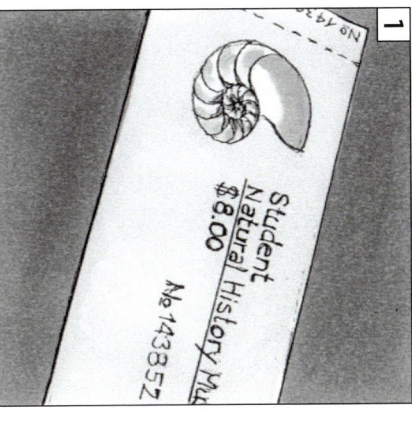

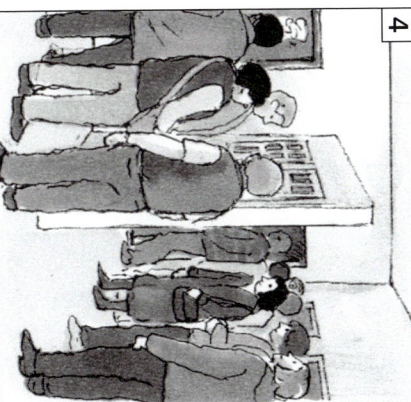

Die richtige Form finden

Notwendige Veränderungen können sein:
- bei Substantiven: Pluralform
- bei Verben: die richtige Zeitform, z.B. **simple present** oder **simple past** (**to walk: he walks ▶ he walked**)
- bei Adjektiven: Adverb (**slow ▶ slowly**) oder Steigerung (**slow ▶ slower ▶ the slowest**)

1 ... to the museum is $8.
2 Let's get our tickets at the ... over there.
3 The museum has a large ... of ... .   ___ / ___
4 The museum is often very ... .
5 A special workshop for children ... every Sunday.
6 You can walk or stand on it.

Can you make a word with the letters from the blue boxes? If you need help, look at sentence 6.

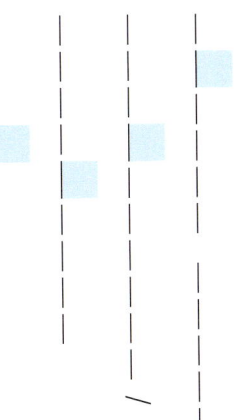

___ /6

Unit 1 | Klassenarbeit A

3 GRAMMAR Life in the city   ___/9

Some friends are talking about their lives in New York. Complete what they say.
*Use **gerunds** of the verbs in the box. Be careful: there are three more verbs than you need.* (6P)

be • go • live • ride • see • shop • take • visit • watch

1 I like _____ photos of all the cool buildings here.
2 I love _____ the museums.
3 My sister and I don't like _____ a bike can be dangerous in Manhattan.
4 _____ in Brooklyn some day.
5 I dream of _____
6 _____ is great in New York. Here you can shop till you drop!

Now you
*What about you? Write three more sentences about living in a town or city. Use **gerunds**.* (3P)

_____

_____

4 GRAMMAR My life in New York   ___/6

Complete these conditional 1 and 2 sentences with the correct form of the verbs in brackets.

1 If I _____ (go) to New York next summer,
   I _____ (watch) the New York Yankees play football.
   I _____ (eat) lots of hamburgers and fries.
   I _____ (not do) much sport, but
   I _____ (watch) a lot of television.

2 If I lived in New York, I _____ (not live) on my own.
   I _____ (live) in an apartment with friends.
   I _____ (go) to the deli every day and
   I _____ (buy) a bagel and a coffee to go.
   I _____ (go) everywhere by subway or bus. I _____ (run) in Central Park once or twice a week. I _____ (see) a Broadway show once a month.

WRITING

A subway story for the school magazine

___/20

You are a student at City High School, New York. You heard the radio programme with the subway stories. Now you want to write your personal story about the subway for the school magazine.
Write 120–150 words.

- Sammle zunächst Ideen (mit einer Mindmap, einer Liste oder den „fünf Ws").
- Überlege dir eine geeignete Überschrift, einen guten Anfang und ein gutes Ende.
- Teile deinen Text in mindestens zwei Absätze ein.
- Schmücke deine Sätze aus mit abwechslungsreicher Wortwahl, Adjektiven, Adverbien usw.
- Schreibe deinen Text im **simple past**.
- Lies deinen Text durch und korrigiere ihn.

Here are some ideas for your story. Use at least four of them:

a parcel • "you've forgotten your parcel" • what could I do? • name on the parcel • telephone number • I got $50

Unit 1
Klassenarbeit B

Gesamtpunktzahl ohne Speaking _____ / 64 Note _____

Gesamtpunktzahl mit Speaking _____ / 84 Note _____

_____ /20

READING

The Empire State Building Run-Up

 Sieh dir vor dem Lesen des Textes Aufgabe 1 an. Überfliege dann den Lesetext. Auf diese Weise bist du schnell dazu in der Lage, die erste Aufgabe zu lösen.

1 The Empire State Building is one of the most famous buildings in the world. Over three million people visit the skyscraper each year to enjoy fantastic views of New York City from the 86th and the 102nd floor Observatories[1]. Every year the building holds a running event[2] called the Empire State Building Run-Up. It's a race where runners run up 1,576 steps to the 86th floor Observatory.

2 The first Empire State Building Run-Up was in 1978 and was the idea of Fred Lebow, President of the New York Road Runners Club. It was part of a project to get more people interested in running. The Empire State Building Run-Up is the most well-known and also the oldest stair race[3]. It's not the only stair race in the world. Other stair races take place in tall buildings across the US, Europe and Asia.

3 Each year about 500 people would like to run in the race but only about 300 can. They have to apply[4] by writing a letter. The New York Road Runners Club then chooses the runners for the race. Although it's not a long-distance[5] race it's a hard race. Runners have to be really fit and give everything to get to the top.

4 The runners come from all over the world. In 2009 a 24-year-old student from Stuttgart, Germany won the race with a time of 10 minutes and 7 seconds. He won the race for the fourth time. A 35-year-old Australian woman living in Singapore won the women's race with a time of 13 minutes and 27 seconds. Her win was quite amazing. Early in the race somebody pushed her to the side. She fell and hurt her left knee and her face. At that time she was in about 20th place and the leader of the race was some floors higher up. It's very difficult to run past other runners while they are running up the stairs, but the Australian woman was able to do it. In the end she was the happy winner. She ended up winning the race by 13 seconds.

[1] observatory (pl observatories) [əbˈzɜːvətri] Aussichtsplattform [2] event [ɪˈvent] Veranstaltung
[3] stair race [ˈsteə(r) reɪs] Treppenlauf [4] (to) apply [əˈplaɪ] sich bewerben [5] long-distance [ˌlɒŋ ˈdɪstəns] Fernstrecken-

1 What is the article about?

Tick (✓) the correct statement.

The article is about …

a) the history of the Empire State Building.
b) a race up the stairs of the Empire State Building.
c) visiting the Empire State Building.
d) fire safety in the Empire State Building.

____/1

2 Missing headings[1]

Match the headings to the paragraphs 1–4.
Be careful: there are two more headings than you need.

A The winners **B** A special place
C Safety **D** How to take part
E Prizes **F** History

| 1 | 2 | 3 | 4 |

____/4

3 About the Run-Up

Match the sentence halves and draw lines to complete the sentences about the article.
Be careful: there are three more endings than you need. (5P)

1 The Empire State Building Run-Up
2 People who would like to run
3 The Run-Up was the idea of
4 About 500 runners
5 It is a hard race, so

a) want to be in the race.
b) and a women's race.
c) is a long-distance race.
d) runners must be really fit.
e) takes place every year.
f) the President of the New York Road Runners Club.
g) four times.
h) have to write a letter to the New York Road Runners Club.

____/8

Now you

Complete the following sentences with information from the text. (3P)

1 Fred Lebow wanted more people _____
2 Not everyone can _____
3 A student has won _____.

[1] heading ['hedɪŋ] *Überschrift*

Unit 1 | Klassenarbeit B

4 Questions about the Run-Up

/7

Mary from San Diego is interested in the race and has a lot of questions. She reads the article about the Empire State Building Run-Up and finds answers to seven of her questions. Tick (✔) the seven questions.

1	When is the next race?
2	How many floors do the runners run up?
3	When was the first race?
4	What are the prizes for the winners?
5	How do the runners train for the race?
6	Are there stair races in other parts of the world?
7	How many people run in the race?
8	How old do you have to be to run in the race?
9	Are the runners only from New York?
10	Is there a women's race?
11	Can I watch the race?
12	Have there been any accidents?

The winner in 2009

LANGUAGE

___/29

1 WORDS American and British English

a) Collect words from Unit 1 that are **different** in American and British English. Write them into the table. (6P)

American English	British English
cellphone	mobile (phone)

b) Write words with a **different spelling** in American and British English into the table. (6P)

American English	British English
center	centre

___/12

2 WORDS In the US

Find three more words from Unit 1 for each word group and add them to the mind map.

```
        buildings
            |
       apartment
            |
        In the US
         /     \
    transport   at the deli
        |          |
     subway      bagel
```

___/9

Unit 1 | Klassenarbeit B   19

Unit 1 | Klassenarbeit B

3 GRAMMAR About sport

These teenagers are talking about sport.
Write sentences about them using the **gerund** and the correct form of the words in brackets. (5P)

____ / 8

1 Sue
"I don't want to play basketball any more."

2 Mike
"I'd like to play football in a big stadium."

3 Alice
"I'd like to play volleyball."

4 Mark
"I'm not a good swimmer."

5 Elly
"I want to do yoga."

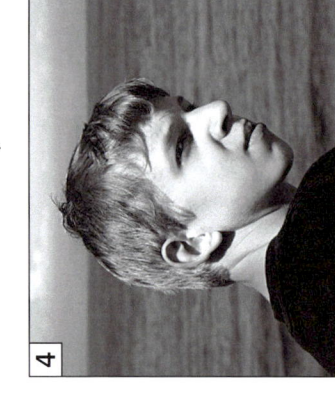
6 Alan
"I run in the school team."

1 Sue _is tired of playing basketball._ (tired of)
2 Mike _____ (dream of)
3 Alice _____ (think of)
4 Mark _____ (not good at)
5 Elly _____ (interested in)
6 Alan _____ (good at)

Now you

What about sport in your life? Write three more sentences about yourself.
One of your sentences must be negative. (3P)

_____
_____

MEDIATION

The Empire State Building

86th Floor Observatory:
The 86th floor Observatory, 1,050 feet (320 meters), reached by high speed, automatic elevators, has two areas: a glass-enclosed area, which is heated in winter and cooled in summer, and a large outdoor area on all four sides of the building. There are high powered binoculars in the outdoor area which visitors can use at a minimal cost. Of course disabled visitors are welcome.

102nd Floor Observatory:
102nd floor Observatory tickets are only sold upon arrival at the Empire State Building at a cost of $15.00 in addition to regular admission tickets.

Observatory Hours:
Open 365 days a year.
8.00 am to 2.00 am. Last elevators go up at 1.15 am.

IMPORTANT: Everyone must go through the security check when entering the building.
Don't bring glass or bottles to the Observatory. Cameras and camcorders are allowed but no tripods.
Please view our Security and Visitor Information for more details.

Admission Prices:

Empire State Building Express Pass	$45
Adults (13–61)	$20
Children (6–12)	$14
Seniors (62+)	$18
Military in uniform	Free
Children (5 or younger – with adult)	Free

ESB Express Pass:
The lines at the Empire State Building Observatory are as well-known as the building itself. There are three different lines. The first one is the security line that everyone must go through. Next comes the ticket line. Visitors who already have tickets need not wait in this line, which can save quite a long time during our busiest times. The third and last line is for the elevators that take you to the Observatory.

Some people have said that it doesn't matter how long you have to wait — the view from the Empire State Building is too awesome to miss. Other people have said that they couldn't visit the Empire State Building Observatory because they just didn't have enough time to see and do everything while in New York City. Now you can. By buying an Express Pass you can always go to the front of each of the three lines.

Need more time for shopping or to see a show? Perhaps there's a restaurant that you just have to experience? The Express Pass is the answer for you. It gives you enough time to do it all in the city that never sleeps.

Unit 1 | Klassenarbeit B

Visiting New York City

👉 Versuche Wörter, die du nicht oder nicht mehr weißt, aus dem Zusammenhang zu erschließen.

Ein Freund deiner Familie möchte nach New York fahren. Während seines Aufenthalts will er ins Empire State Building. Er war auf der Website, aber da sein Englisch nicht so gut ist, bittet er dich, ihm die wichtigsten Informationen zu den folgenden Themen mitzuteilen:

1 Informationen über die Aussichtsplattform im 86. Stockwerk *(mindestens 5 Hinweise)* (5P)

2 Informationen über die Eintrittskarten für die Aussichtsplattform im 102. Stockwerk (wo man sie bekommt, wie viel sie kosten) (2P)

3 Öffnungszeiten der Aussichtsplattformen (Abendöffnungszeit: wie lange, was gibt es zu beachten?) (3P)

4 Informationen über den Empire State Building Express Pass (Preis, warum es den Pass gibt und der Vorteil des Passes) (4P)

5 Gibt es einen Vorteil, wenn man bereits eine Eintrittskarte hat? (1P)

SPEAKING

02 A street interview ___/20

Every year millions of people visit New York. To find out what they like and don't like about the city, the New York Tourist Organization asks people to take part in street interviews.

Listen to an interview with a Spanish visitor.

> 👉 Höre dir das Interview an und notiere die Formulierungen, die hilfreich sein könnten, wenn du im **Now you** selbst an einem Interview teilnimmst.

Interviewer	Hello, can I ask you a few questions?
You	…
Interviewer	Can you tell me a bit about yourself?
You	…
Interviewer	Are you here on vacation or on business?
You	…
Interviewer	Where are you staying in New York City? And how long are you staying for?
You	…
Interviewer	Are you here on your own?
You	…
Interviewer	How long have you been here and what have you seen?
You	…
Interviewer	What kind of transport have you used here in New York?
You	…
Interviewer	So what do you like about New York?
You	…
Interviewer	Is there anything that you don't like?
You	…
Interviewer	Will you come to New York again?
You	…
Interviewer	Thanks for your time. Have a nice day!

03 Now you

You are visiting New York and are taking part in a street interview. Press "Pause" after each question and give your answer.

Unit 2

Klassenarbeit A

Gesamtpunktzahl ohne Speaking _____ /57 Note _____

Gesamtpunktzahl mit Speaking _____ /75 Note _____

LISTENING

_____ /11

🎧 04 **Which is the best school trip – Yosemite National Park or San Diego?**

Class 8B and their teacher Mrs Astbury from Goldwater High School in Phoenix, Arizona are talking about their school trip. One group wants to go to Yosemite National Park, another group wants to go on a trip to San Diego, California.

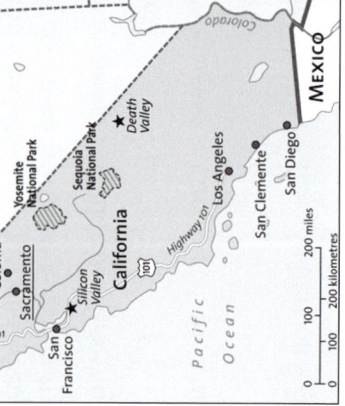

_____ /4

1 The San Diego presentation

Look at the pictures. Listen to the text and put the four activities in the order they are talked about. Be careful: there is one more picture than you need. (4P)

New words
ghost tour [ɡəʊst tʊə(r)] Geistertour

A

B

C

D

E

2 Who in the class?

Listen again and tick (✓) the correct answer.

1	The first group ...	a) has already given a presentation.	
		b) thinks Yosemite National Park is boring.	
		c) has talked about a climbing tour.	
		d) wants to stay in a hostel.	

2	The teacher ...	a) has visited Yosemite National Park.	
		b) talks about last week's presentation.	
		c) wants to go to San Diego.	
		d) doesn't like the second presentation.	

3	The second group ...	a) wants to arrive in San Diego in the evening.	
		b) wants to go on a special guided tour.	
		c) wants to go to the beach on the last day of the trip.	
		d) wants to go on a 30-minute boat trip.	

4	The class ...	a) thinks San Diego is too far.	
		b) has no questions about the San Diego trip.	
		c) can't decide.	
		d) has to decide on Tuesday.	

___/4

3 Things to do

The second group will have to do some organizing if the class decides to go to San Diego.
Make notes about three of the jobs they talk about.

To do list

School Trip to San Diego

___/3

Unit 2 | Klassenarbeit A

LANGUAGE

_____ / 31

1 WORDS Questions about the trip to San Diego

_____ / 8

The students are talking about the trip to San Diego. Complete their sentences with words from the box.
Be careful: there are three more words than you need.

> attractions • business • disadvantages • experience • governor
> homeless • legal • minority • Pacific Ocean • population • products

1 Is San Diego close to the _____?
2 I know about the zoo, but what other _____ of San Diego? It's a big city, right?
3 What is the _____ people in San Diego?
4 Are there many _____ of going to San Diego?
5 Are there any _____ of California?
6 San Diego is in California. Who is the _____ of California?
7 What _____ are made in San Diego?
8 Do you think that the people who want to go to San Diego are in the _____?

2 WORDS Who or what is it?

_____ / 5

Look at the pictures and complete the sentences with the new words from Unit 2.

1

2

3

4

5

1 Wine is made from _____.

2 A _____ is between two countries.

3 A _____ does a lot of sport.

4 A _____ is someone who works in a garden.

5 A _____ doesn't eat meat.

3 GRAMMAR Facts about California

a) *The class is talking about California. Complete the sentences with the passive. (6P)*

> **The passive: simple present**
> Bildung: **am/are/is + past participle** (3. Form des Verbs)
>
> is + past participle
>
> A lot of wine   is   produced.
>
> are + past participle
>
> Strawberries   are   grown   in California.

1 A lot of films _____ (make) in Hollywood.

2 San Francisco _____ (name) after Francis of Assisi[1].

3 Even today gold _____ (find) in California.

4 Oranges _____ (grow) in California.

5 California _____ (know) for its endless beaches.

6 Universal Studios in Hollywood _____ (visit) by many tourists every year.

b) *Answer the questions below about your area. You can use the ideas in the boxes to help you. (3P)*

1 What is your area known for? | church, castle, cathedral, festival, river |

2 What is made there? | cars, machines, wine, cheese |

3 What is grown there? | potatoes, apples, strawberries |

_____

_____

_____

[1] Francis of Assisi *Franz von Assisi*

Unit 2 | Klassenarbeit A

4 GRAMMAR The school trip

___/9

a) *Complete the sentences about the San Diego presentation with the **passive**.* (6P)

> **The passive: simple past**
> Bildung: **was/were + past participle** (3. Form des Verbs)
>
> | | was + past participle | |
> |---|---|---|
> | A lot of wine | was produced | last year. |
>
> | | were + past participle | |
> |---|---|---|
> | 700,000 tons of strawberries | were grown | in California last year. |

1 Four students _____ (choose) to present their ideas.

2 A lot of photos _____ (show) to the class.

3 A map _____ (draw) on the board.

4 Two different activities _____ (speak) about for the last day of the trip.

5 The zoo tour _____ (describe) well.

6 The class _____ (ask) to decide on the school trip later.

b) *Imagine you are describing a presentation that you gave.*
*Write three sentences using the passive and verbs from **a**).* (3P)

Example:
A topic was chosen.

_____

_____

_____

MEDIATION

Come on our ghost tour

Markieren des Textes
Sieh dir die Aufgabenstellung vor dem Lesen an. Markiere dir beim Lesen des Textes bereits die Informationen, die für die Lösung notwendig sind. Du kannst je nach Aufgabe auch verschiedene Farben verwenden. Das erleichtert dir den Überblick.

Would you like to meet real ghosts and learn their stories? Then come on our ghost tour to hear the scary and tragic stories of people who lived here one or two centuries ago. Meet Jim who was hanged for stealing a rowboat in 1852. Hear Anna crying for her lost children. These are some of the sad stories of people who lived in California long ago.

You will be led around by a "Ghost Hunter" who doesn't seem to see the ghosts that our visitors always see. Learn San Diego's sad stories and meet real ghosts who have come back to tell their stories in a funny and spooky way.

Tours are limited to 50 people. Two tours are offered every Friday and Saturday night. The first tour begins at 6.30 pm and the second tour begins at 7.00 pm. We ask you to arrive at the Visitor Information Center about 15 minutes before the start of the tour.

Information

Tour Name:
Ghost Tours

Event Dates:
Friday and Saturday evenings

Event Times:
6.30 pm and 7.00 pm.

Cost:
Adults: $10 per ticket, children under 13: $5. Special prices are offered on the first and second Friday of every month but only for the first tour beginning at 6.30 pm. These prices are for groups with at least 12 persons only. Reservations for these offers can only be made on the internet at the Brown Paper Tickets agency.

Tour Length:
1 hour

Tickets:
Visitor Information Center at Old Town San Diego State Historic Park. Tickets are only sold on the day of the tour on a first-come-first-served basis.

Reservations:
www.brownpapertickets/events

Information:
619-220-5422

Webpage:
www.parks.ca.gov/oldtownsandiego

Du bist mit deiner Familie im Urlaub in San Diego, Kalifornien. Dort triffst du Frau Andrea Schiffbauer aus Düsseldorf. Sie hat den Flyer über die Geistertouren von der Tourist Information bekommen. Da sie einiges darin nicht versteht, bittet sie dich um Hilfe.

Unit 2 | Klassenarbeit A

Lies den Flyer auf S. 29 und schreibe eine kurze Zusammenfassung der wichtigsten Informationen zu den folgenden Themen:

1 Allgemeines:
- was die „Ghost Tour" ist,
- was das Besondere an der Führung ist,
- Uhrzeiten der Führungen,
- Preise usw. *(mindestens 6 Details)*.

2 Reservierung:
- Frau Schiffbauer möchte eine Führung für ihre Gruppe (von 15 Erwachsenen) organisieren. Sage ihr, wie sie an Tickets kommen kann und was sie kosten.

SPEAKING

05 Getting information on the phone ___/18

The students have agreed on the school trip to San Diego. Today they are working on the programme for the trip. One student rings up a surf school in San Diego to find out more about surf lessons. Listen to the phone call.

Höre dir die Fragen und Antworten der Schülerin genau an.
Sie helfen dir, wenn du in **Now you** die Rolle eines Schülers oder einer Schülerin übernimmst.
Falls du etwas nicht verstehst, höre den Abschnitt noch mal an.
Wenn du mehr Hilfe benötigst, findest du den Hörtext im Lösungsheft.

06 Now you

Imagine you are planning a visit to San Diego Zoo for your school trip. Phone the zoo and ask for information.

1   San Diego Zoo: ▼

You: Sage, wer du bist und dass du von der Kennedy High School anrufst.
Sage, dass du mit deiner Klasse nach San Diego kommst und den Zoo besuchen möchtest. (3P)

2   San Diego Zoo: ▼

You: Bejahe die Frage und sage, dass eure Klassenfahrt vom 2.–5. Mai sein wird. (2P)

3   San Diego Zoo: ▼

You: Frage nach den Öffnungszeiten des Zoos. (1P)

4   San Diego Zoo: ▼

You: Frage, ob der Zoo eine Führung speziell für Schulklassen hat. (1P)

5   San Diego Zoo: ▼

You: Sage, dass du in der 8. Klasse bist und dass ihr 30 Leute sein werdet: 28 Jugendliche und zwei Erwachsene. (3P)

6   San Diego Zoo: ▼

You: Sage, dass das großartig klingt und frage, wie viel Zeit man für diese Führung benötigt. (2P)

7   San Diego Zoo: ▼

You: Frage, um wie viel Uhr die Führungen beginnen. (1P)

8   San Diego Zoo: ▼

You: Du bist einverstanden. Frage, wie viel die Tour für die ganze Gruppe kostet und ob es eine Gruppenermäßigung gibt. (3P)

9   San Diego Zoo: ▼

You: Sage, dass du erst mit deiner Lehrerin und der Klasse sprechen musst.
Sage, dass du dich morgen wieder meldest. Verabschiede dich. (2P)

10   San Diego Zoo:

Unit 2
Klassenarbeit B

Gesamtpunktzahl ____ /57   Note ____

____ /11

READING

"Earthquakes: we want to be prepared"
San Jose High School, San Diego gets prepared for earthquakes

By our reporter Jack Simon

1
This year San Jose High School will take part in[1] the earthquake safety exercise that is held all over California on the third Thursday of October every year. "Our school safety team is going to plan the activities," says head teacher Mr Nicola. "Here in California we're living in earthquake country, that's why parents, teachers and students have agreed on being part of earthquake safety day or "ESD" as it's called. We want to be prepared when the next earthquake comes."

2
The school's safety team has twelve members: parents, students and teachers. The safety team has met several times to work out a program for the big day in October. "Today we don't know yet what the exercises on ESD will look like exactly," says Mrs Cast, teacher and member of the team. "But an important part of the exercise will be finding out how you can protect yourself in case of an earthquake, and to actually practice it. A second part will be to get all of our 850 students to walk quietly out of the school building without panicking."

3
A first step was to ask parents to bring an "earthquake bag" for their children to school. The "earthquake bag" should contain two bottles of water, two snacks, a card with the family contact information and a family photo. Parents may add one or two other things that they think might help their children in case of an earthquake. And the child's name must be clearly written on the bag. "At the end of the school year the bags will be returned – hopefully they will be unused[2]," says Mr Nicola.

4
In the weeks before the exercise in October the teachers at San Jose High School will talk about earthquakes with their students. "There'll be different topics for the different age groups: stories, games and quizzes for the younger students, surfing the internet and writing reports for the older ones," explains Mr Nicola. By the end of their time at San Jose every student will know a lot about earthquakes worldwide and especially in California. "We hope that with our activities we will help more people to survive an earthquake," says Mr Nicola.

5
This report shows you – our readers – another good example of how people in California are trying to live with the dangers of earthquakes. We hope that this article makes you, your school or your office think about what you could do. Why don't you join in and become part of the Californian program or start a program of your own?

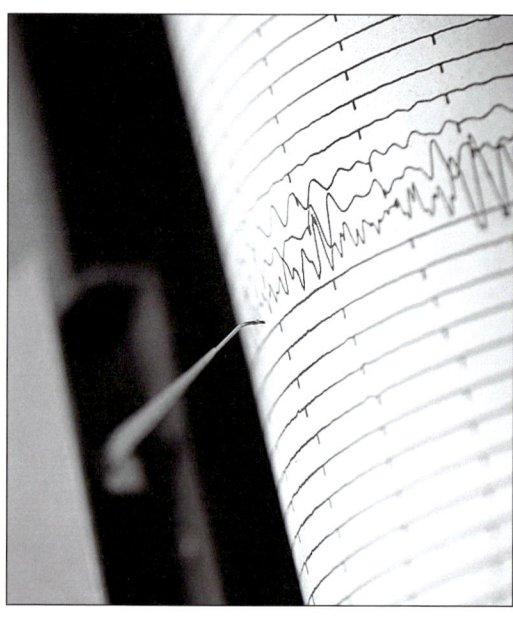

[1] (to) take part in [teɪk pɑːt ɪn] *teilnehmen an*   [2] unused [ʌnˈjuːzd] *unbenutzt*

Unit 2 | Klassenarbeit B

1 Headings¹

Write headings for at least three of the paragraphs of the newspaper article.

☞ Überschriften sind in der Regel kurz formuliert und keine ganzen Sätze.
Die Überschrift gibt eine kurze Vorschau auf die Kernaussage eines Abschnittes.

_____

_____

_____

___/3

2 FAQ

San Jose High School's website has some FAQ (frequently asked questions²) about the school's earthquake safety day (ESD).
Answer the questions with information from the newspaper article. You do not need to write complete sentences.

1 When is ESD?

2 How often is ESD?

3 Why is there an ESD at San Jose High School?

4 Who can be on the safety team?

5 What is the safety team's job?

6 What happens on ESD? (two things)

7 What can parents do?

8 What classroom activities are being organized?

___/8

---

¹ heading ['hedɪŋ] *Überschrift*   ² frequently asked questions ['fri:kwəntli ɑ:skt 'kwestʃənz] *häufig gestellte Fragen*

33

Unit 2 | Klassenarbeit B

_____ /26
_____ /10

LANGUAGE

1 WORDS A safety team meeting

Here are some statements from the members of the safety team.
Complete the sentences with words from the box. Be careful: there are three more words than you need.

act • advantages • attitude • change • except • experience • majority
make sure • member • offer • specific • whatever • whoever

1 It is important that the students' _____ towards earthquakes changes.

2 The _____ of our students have already brought their earthquake bags to school.

3 The earthquake safety exercises mean that the students will know what to do if we _____ an earthquake.

4 We need to _____ students a realistic experience of an earthquake.

5 _____ visits our school on ESD should be part of the exercises.

6 After ESD we must meet again and talk about what we need to _____ next year.

7 We should _____ that all parents know about ESD.

8 We must give parents _____ information about the activities on ESD.

9 After ESD every student will know how to _____ in an earthquake.

10 _____ happens, I think that ESD will be a success.

2 Getting by in English

Write what you would say in English.

Was sagst du, wenn du …

1. jemandem sagen willst, dass du gut mit deiner Schwester auskommst?

   _____

2. sagen willst, „keine Panik"?

   _____

3. sagen willst, dass eine Sache am Ende gut ausgehen wird?

   _____

4. fragen willst, ob du einen Blick auf das Buch werfen kannst?

   _____

5. fragen willst, welches Land das wärmste auf der Erde ist?

   _____

6. sagen willst, dass manche Leute immer noch Vorurteile gegenüber Minderheiten haben?

   _____

___/6

3 GRAMMAR San Jose High School and ESD

*A student from San Jose High School is writing about ESD. Fill in the correct form of the verbs in the **simple past**. Be careful: some of the sentences are active, some are passive.*

👉 **Active and passive sentences in the simple past**
active: He **brought** his earthquake bag to school.
passive: The earthquake bag **was brought** to school.

The day before ESD, we _____ (ask) to bring our earthquake bags to school. I took my bag to school, and everyone in the class _____ (tell) to keep their earthquake bags with them at all times because you never know when there could be an earthquake. At 9.30 am the school bell rang and the ESD exercises _____ (begin). Everyone _____ (do) the exercises: teachers and students. When the bell rang, everybody _____ (tell) to get on the floor under a table or desk. We waited on the floor for a few minutes until a sign _____ (give). Then we all _____ (stand up). The bell rang again and everyone _____ (leave) the building quietly. Outside the building all the students _____ (count). When the head teacher was sure that no one was left in the building, we _____ (tell) to go back to our classes.

___/10

Unit 2 | Klassenarbeit B

35

WRITING

An e-mail to California

Your penfriend[1] in California has written you an e-mail and told you about earthquake safety day at his/her school. He/She wants to know if you have anything like it at your school in Germany.

Write about 120 words and tell him/her:

– that there are fire exercises at your school,
– about the fire exercises (when in the school year, how often, do students know the date?, special things, …),
– your opinion of the exercise.
Ask your penfriend a question.

[1] penfriend ['penfrend]   *Brieffreund/in*

Klassenarbeit A

Unit 3

Gesamtpunktzahl ____ /101 Note ____

LISTENING

🔊07 **Burger day**

Listen to this announcement at an American high school about a healthy burger project.

1 The best poster

Look at the posters, then listen to the text. Which of the three posters **best** represents the school's special activity? Choose one.

 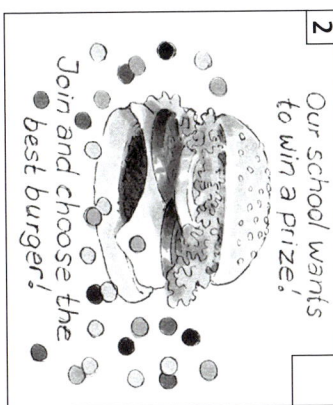 

1   2   3

____ /1

2 About the announcement

Read the following sentences. Then listen to the text again and tick (✓) the correct box.

1 The school	a) has already started with the health programme.	
	b) wants to sell fresh fruit in the next project.	
	c) has already won a prize.	
2 The head teacher	a) explains why the school has started this project.	
	b) explains why the teachers are organizing this project.	
	c) explains why burgers are not good for the students.	
3 The students in class 8	a) have tested lots of different healthy burgers.	
	b) have already chosen their favourite healthy burger.	
	c) have made some healthy burgers.	
4 The students	a) can test the burgers after the announcement.	
	b) can test four burgers in their lunch break.	
	c) can test as many burgers as they want in their lunch break.	
5 The test burgers	a) come in different sizes.	
	b) are smaller than normal ones.	
	c) come with a whole-grain roll.	

____ /8

37

Unit 3 | Klassenarbeit A

6	The difference between the four burgers is that	a) two are vegetarian and two are with meat.
		b) they don't have the same things on top.
		c) they are made by different classes.
7	The students are asked to choose their favourite burger by	a) putting all their stickers on the poster they like best.
		b) putting their stickers on only one poster.
		c) putting their stickers on one poster or on different posters.
8	The head teacher	a) is looking forward to seeing class 8 again.
		b) is looking forward to the testing between 12 and 1.
		c) is looking forward to helping his school.

____ / 59

____ / 12

LANGUAGE

1 WORDS A food mind map

The students are talking about food in their health class. Write the missing group words into the blue bubbles and find the words on the lines.

☞ Du kannst in dieser Mindmap weitere Äste ergänzen und noch mehr Punkte sammeln.

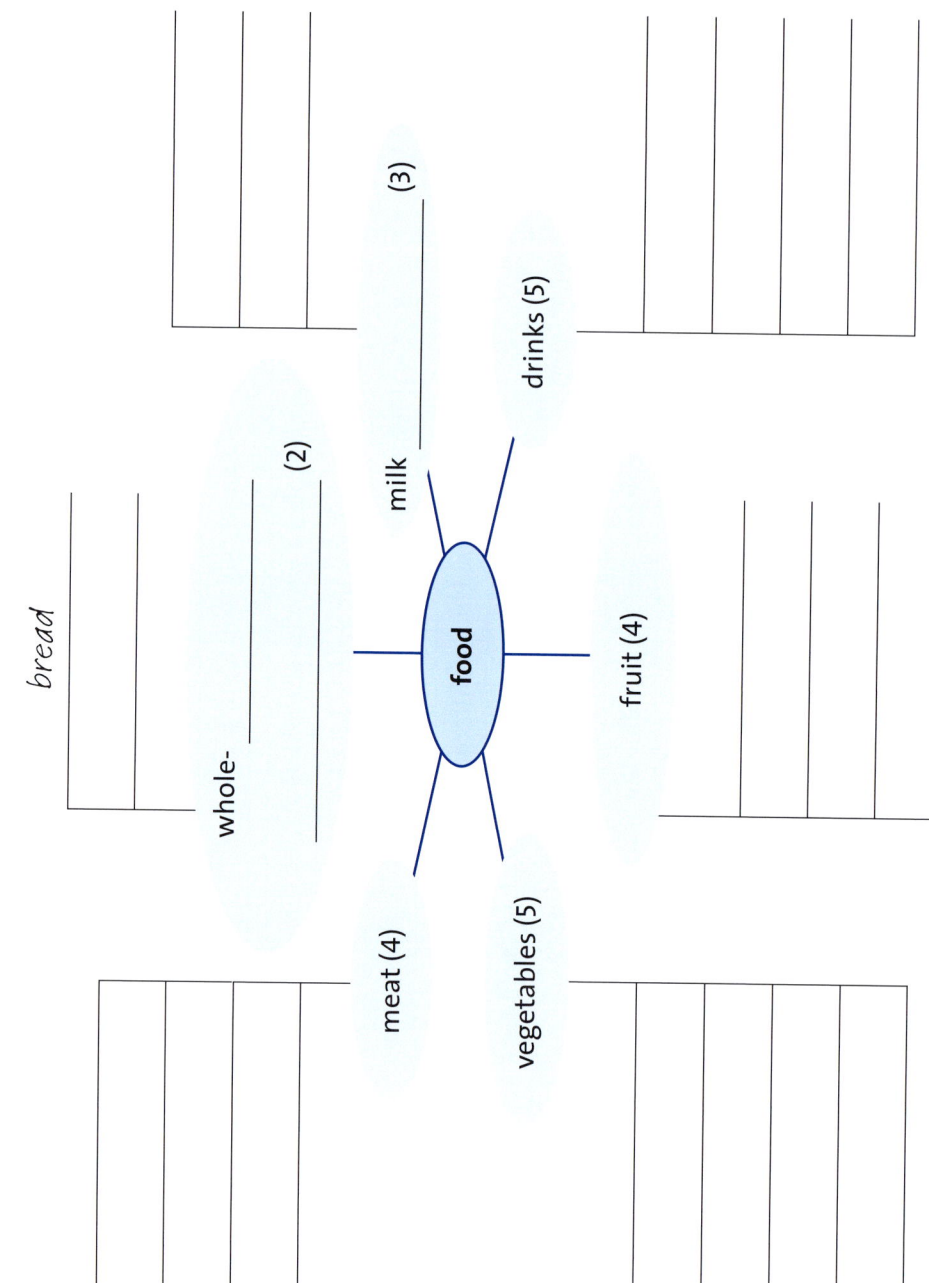

2 WORDS We are a healthy school

___/12

Complete the sentences and fill in the crossword. The letters in the blue boxes will tell you what you should eat two or three times a day.

We believe that a healthy school is a better school. We are sure that **1** … kids study better. At our school students get **2** … fruit in our **3** … every day. Our students have also made a healthy burger that **4** … fewer **5** … than the **6** … burger. We believe that sport is very important for our students. That's why we make sure that they get daily **7** …. They can be **8** … after every second **9** …. We offer lots of different **10** …. The school's **11** … team is very successful and lots of the girls are **12** …. Come and see our school!

1 __ __
2 __ __ __
3 __ __ __
4 __ __
5 __ __

3 GRAMMAR Food words

___/10

Look at the food words in the box and write them into the correct list.

egg • milk • tomato • whole-grain product
water • cheese • tea • meat • apple • lemon

Countable nouns a/an, one	Uncountable nouns some

Unit 3 | Klassenarbeit A

39

Unit 3 | Klassenarbeit A

4 GRAMMAR Our healthy meals

___ /6

The school cafeteria has prepared some healthy meals. Look at the posters and complete the sentences below.

1 Meal 1 is a healthy _____ with some _____, two _____ and an _____.

2 Meal 2 is some _____, some _____, two _____, some _____ and a _____.

3 Meal 3 is a _____, some _____, some more _____ and some _____.

👉 **Zählbare und nicht zählbare Nomen**
Countable nouns sind zählbare Nomen. Es gibt sie im Singular und Plural. Wenn du „wie viele?" fragst, kannst du die bezeichneten Dinge zählen (**a book – two books**).
Uncountable nouns bezeichnen Dinge, die du nicht zählen kannst. Hierzu gehören Lebensmittel (**some bread, butter, milk**) und abstrakte Begriffe (**some furniture, homework, information**).

5 GRAMMAR The health lesson

___ /4

*Here are some statements which the students and teacher made in the last health lesson. Read the sentences and add **the** where necessary.*

1 We know that _____ young people often eat _____ fast food.

2 We are proud that _____ burgers that _____ students of class 8 made are really healthy.

3 Lots of _____ people work so much that they aren't able to cook.

4 Then they often eat _____ fast food and don't prepare their own meals.

5 Many people say that _____ burgers sold in fast food restaurants are a quick and cheap lunch.

6 I don't like burgers. My favourite dish is _____ spaghetti that my sister often makes.

👉 **Mit oder ohne „the"?**
Prüfe: Sind die Nomen näher bestimmt, z. B. durch eine **of**-Fügung, einen Relativsatz oder eine Ortsangabe? I really like **the teachers at my school**. Oder sind die Nomen allgemein gebraucht? **Life** is exciting at the moment.

6 GRAMMAR Our burger project

The students in class 8 talk about one day during their healthy burger project. Complete the sentences. Use the **simple past** or the **past perfect**.

After we _____ (find) a lot of information on the internet, we _____ (talk) about it. When we _____ (discuss) the healthy burgers for more than an hour, we _____ (decide) it was time to try and make some. After we _____ (write) the shopping list, we _____ (go) to the supermarket. In the lunch break we _____ (try) the different burgers which we _____ (prepare) in the school's kitchen. They _____ (be) all delicious.

☞ **Simple past** oder **past perfect**?

Was geschah? ▶ Du benutzt **simple past** für abgeschlossene Ereignisse in der Vergangenheit.
Was geschah zuerst? ▶ Du benutzt **past perfect**, um auszudrücken, dass etwas vor etwas anderem in der Vergangenheit passiert ist (Vorvergangenheit).
Beispiel: After we <u>had prepared</u> the burgers, we <u>ate</u> them.

Now you

Write about things that you or another person did after you or another person had done something else. Use the **simple past** and the **past perfect**. Write three sentences. (6P)

1 After I _____
   I _____.

2 _____
   _____.

3 _____
   _____.

____/15

Unit 3 | Klassenarbeit A

MEDIATION

 ___ /13

Da diese Übung eine zusätzliche Mediation-Aufgabe ist, wird sie in der Gesamtpunktzahl für Klassenarbeit A nicht gewertet!

Fruit makes school meals healthier

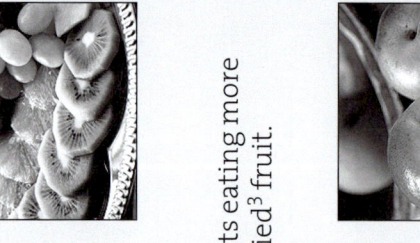

Adding fruit to your school meals is a great way to make them healthier, and the kids will love the change too. People who eat fruit every day have less chance of getting ill, and fruit helps students to work better at school. Here are some ideas to help you to change your school menus for the better.

It's easy to add fruit to school meals. We like to add oranges, apples or grapes to salads so that the students get as many vitamins as possible. Try offering fruit at the right time of year. Apples are great in October (our teenagers love baked apples¹ as desserts!), but in June strawberries are delicious and of course they're cheaper then too. If you plan well, you can save your school money.

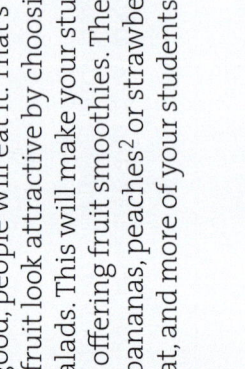

Everyone knows that if food looks good, people will eat it. That's why presentation is so important. Make fruit look attractive by choosing fruit with different colors for fruit salads. This will make your students interested in the food. You could try offering fruit smoothies. These are delicious with milk or yoghurt and bananas, peaches² or strawberries. Cutting fruit up makes it easier to eat, and more of your students will be interested in trying new things.

Break time snacks are another chance to get students eating more fruit. You can offer fresh fruit cut up into pieces or dried³ fruit. Both are better than chocolate!

Finally, when you're preparing fruit for your school meals it's important to remember to wash everything (even melons and oranges) before you start. You should dry⁴ the fruit after you have washed it too.

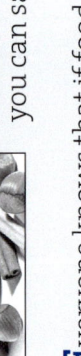

A health project

Deine Schule hat beschlossen, eine „gesunde" Schule zu werden. Deine Projektgruppe kümmert sich um gesundes Essen. Du willst Informationen, die du im Internet gefunden hast, in deine Gruppe einbringen. Notiere Stichpunkte zu den Fragen auf Deutsch in dein Lernheft.

a) *Warum ist es wichtig, Obst zu essen?* (2P)

b) *Fasse die drei Hauptideen zusammen und gib jeweils mindestens zwei Beispiele, wie sie umgesetzt werden können.* (9P)

c) *Wie soll man das Obst vorbereiten?* (2P)

¹ baked apple [ˌbeɪktˈæpl] *Bratapfel*   ² peach [piːtʃ] *Pfirsich*
³ dry (adj.) [draɪ] *trocken – dried getrocknet*   ⁴ (to) dry sth. *abtrocknen*

STUDY SKILLS

Our school burger

Last month it was burger testing day at our school. Our school wants to become a healthier school, in fact, we want to win a prize: the Healthiest School in Missouri. Our head teacher says that if the students eat healthily, they'll get better grades. It's an exciting project!

Burger testing day was organized by class 8. They wanted to make a healthy burger for our school and had prepared four different burgers for us to test.

At lunch break on burger testing day I went to take part in the testing with my friends Sue and Lucy. "It's a good thing I'm so hungry," said Lucy, when we arrived at the cafeteria, "I hope the burgers are really big!" Sue said she wasn't so hungry because she'd eaten an apple at break. "Lunch is a very important meal, Sue," I said, laughing.

So, we arrived and each of us was given a plate with bits of burger on to test. Each burger had a number. "Let's look at the burgers before we start," I said. "Then we can guess which one will be our favorite." So, we had a good look and Lucy and I chose number three, Sue said she liked number four.

"Right, let's get started. I'm really hungry," said Lucy. "Why don't we make notes so we don't forget important facts," Sue asked. We agreed and each of us started testing a different burger. For a few minutes we didn't say anything, we were really thinking about the burgers, like food experts on the television!

After I had tried all four burgers, I was sure which was my favorite. It was number four. I love beefburgers, and the baked potato chips on top were really delicious. Sue and Lucy couldn't decide. Sue liked the vegetarian burger and the chicken burger. "They're both very healthy and they taste[1] awesome," she said. "The vegetarian burger tastes as good as it looks." I didn't agree with Sue. I didn't like the vegetarian burger. Lucy said she liked them all except number two, the beefburger. "I hate onions!" she told us. Luckily for Sue and Lucy you could choose more than one burger, so they didn't have to choose just one!

At the end of the day there was an announcement from the head teacher. Burger number 4, the beefburger with the baked potato chips on top, my favorite burger, was our new school burger!

Over the next few months, as part of the healthy school project, our school organized other projects too. Class 5 designed a salad bar, and it was decided to take out all the vending machines[2] from the school. Lucy, Sue and I wanted to see if eating healthily really did make a difference to our grades. We stopped eating chocolate and biscuits and started eating more fruit. We visited the salad bar every day and ate healthy main meals like "my" school burger. Lucy found it really hard, because she loves eating, but we all worked together. And guess what! At the end of the school year we all got better grades. In fact, I was top of the class!

---

1 (to) taste [teɪst] *schmecken* 2 vending machine [ˈvendɪŋməˌʃiːn] *Automat*

Unit 3 | Klassenarbeit A

Writing a summary

Read the story and summarize it.

a) Mark the most important events of the story: who did what when, where and why?

b) Write about ten sentences in your exercise book.
You can start like this:

- The story is about ...
- The school ...
- Class 8 ...
- Three girls ...
- First ...
- Then ...

👉 Wichtige Punkte für die Inhaltsangabe

- Sie ist kürzer als der Originaltext.
- Einleitung: Wovon handelt der Text (ein bis zwei Sätze)?
- Die wichtigsten Ereignisse nennen: Wer hat was, wann, wo und warum gemacht?
- Schreibe im **simple present** und in eigenen Worten.
- Verwende keine direkte Rede, nenne keine Beispiele!

Klassenarbeit B

Unit 3

Gesamtpunktzahl ohne Speaking ____ /72 Note ____

Gesamtpunktzahl mit Speaking ____ /92 Note ____

READING

A letter from Hermann

Jason is a 15-year-old student from Hermann. He has written this letter to the head teacher of a school in Bad Arolsen.

____ /19

167 Wine Street
Hermann
65041 MO
USA
March 25

Dear Sir or Madam[1],

I'm a student in grade 9 at Hermann High School, Missouri, USA. I'm 15 years old and I'm interested in doing an exchange with a school in Germany next year. I thought you might be able to help me. Maybe there's a student at your school who is interested in taking part in an exchange and would like to come to Hermann. I live together with my mom and dad and my two little sisters, Anna and Lucy. They're five and eight years old. My parents have a hotel in Hermann, and we have a lot of German speaking guests. I'd like to be better at German so that I can talk more with the guests and help my parents with German e-mails and letters. At school my favorite subjects are Science and Math. In my free time I like cooking for my family and friends — I make a great lasagne! I also play baseball in the school team. Here at my school we have a German club, which I joined two years ago. I can understand easy German conversations quite well. Coming to Germany would mean that I could learn lots more German and find out more about German people. I'm looking for an exchange partner who is about my age. He/She doesn't have to have the same hobbies as me, but what's important is that we are both open to new experiences! I'm interested in the history of Germany and would love to visit Berlin while I'm on the exchange. It would be good if my partner was interested in going there as well. I'd like to come to Germany from September to February and I thought that my exchange partner could come to Hermann from March to August. Of course, we can talk more about the dates later on. I hope I have the chance to come to Bad Arolsen next school year, and my family and I are really looking forward to welcoming a German student to Hermann.

Thank you for your help.

Yours,
Jason Winter

[1] Dear Sir or Madam [dɪəˈsɜː; ɔːˈmædəm] Sehr geehrte Damen und Herren

Unit 3 | Klassenarbeit B

1 About the letter

___ /4

There are no paragraphs in the text. Use a pen and add four paragraphs to mark the structure of the letter. Your paragraphs should answer these questions:

a) Who is the writer and why is he writing?
b) What does he say about his family and what is he interested in?
c) What is he looking for and what are his plans?
d) How does he end his letter?

2 A notice for the school's notice board

___ /15

The head teacher has asked you to write a notice for the school's notice board. Fill in the missing information. Use key words.

1 **Name, age, where from** (4 facts)   Jason Winter, 15 years old, from Hermann, Missouri

2 **Family** (2 facts)
  • **what his parents do**   _____
  • **brothers and sisters**   _____

3 **Details about school** (2 facts)
  • **grade**   _____
  • **favourite subjects**   _____

4 **About his German** (2 facts)   _____

5 **Hobbies** (2 facts)   _____

6 **Reasons for exchange** (3 facts)   _____

7 **When (dates)** (2 facts)   _____

8 **If interested, please contact** (1 fact)   _____

LANGUAGE

1 WORDS The Winters are discussing the exchange

____ /21

Before Jason decided to write the letter to the school in Germany, the Winters talked about the exchange. Read the dialogue and fill in the missing words. Choose from the box. Be careful: there are four more words than you need.

| (to) be allowed • bulletin board • (to) compare • classes foreign • (to) get involved in • grades • period sister city • (to) study • system • traditions • worried |

Mr Winter Well Jason, let's talk about your idea of doing an exchange. The German school _____ is different to ours, so you might have some difficulties when you come back. You'll have different _____ to your classes here in Hermann. I think you'll have _____ a lot more than you're doing at the moment to keep your _____.

Jason You're probably right, Dad. But staying in Germany will be really good for me. My German will be excellent, I'll know a lot about German _____, which will help us with the hotel when we have _____ guests who speak German.

Mrs Winter I think we need to talk about the German exchange partner. Where could we find a nice boy? What about Hermann's _____ Bad Arolsen?

Jason Good idea, Mom. But I can write to other schools too. They can put a notice up on the school's _____. I'm sure there'll be students who want _____ an exchange.

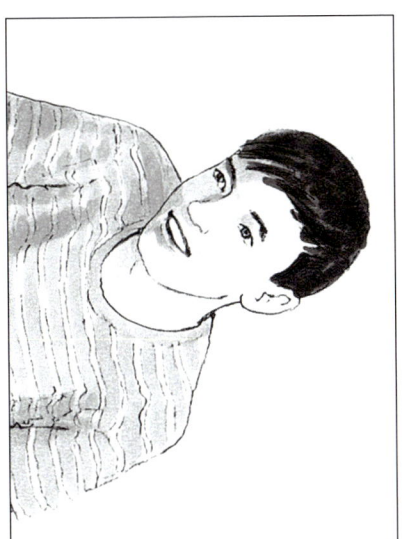

____ /9

Unit 3 | Klassenarbeit B

2 GRAMMAR At my German school

*Emily has written about her exchange year in Stuttgart. Add **the** where you need it.*

___ /7

When I lived in Stuttgart, ____ school played an important part in my daily life. I really liked ____ school I went to. Usually in ____ Germany ____ lessons start very early in the morning but ____ lessons at my school didn't start before 8.30. Lucky me! ____ History was my favorite class.

I'm interested in ____ history, especially in ____ history of Germany after the Second World War.

I didn't really miss much about ____ US while I was there. But one thing I did miss was ____ extracurricular sports activities at school. The Germans like ____ sport, but they don't have school teams. If you want to play ____ sport, you have to join a club. If you like ____ soccer, you can watch matches every Saturday afternoon. I often went to watch VFB Stuttgart, ____ local team, play.

3 GRAMMAR Thoughts and questions about the exchange

___ /5

Other students are interested in the exchange.
*Complete the students' thoughts and questions with **much** and **many**.*

1 I want to have as ____ information as possible before I decide.
2 How ____ students can go on the exchange to Germany this year?
3 How ____ money will I need?
4 Will we have to do ____ work to prepare for the exchange?
5 I found ____ interesting articles written by exchange students on the internet.

👉 **Much oder many?**
Many heißt „viele" und steht nur mit Nomen im Plural: How **many students** are in your class?
Much heißt „viel" und steht nur mit nicht zählbaren Nomen: How **much bread** is left?

WRITING

👉 Briefe schreiben

- Lies noch einmal den Brief von Jason im Lösungsheft auf S. 30.
- Gliedere deinen Antwort-Brief in **Absätze**:
  Schreibe in der Einleitung, wer du bist und warum du schreibst.
  Teile mehr über dich mit, z. B. deine Interessen oder Lieblingsfächer.
  Stelle Fragen oder beantworte die Fragen deines Brieffreundes.
  Achte auf einen freundlichen Schluss, z. B. **I look forward to hearing from you.**

A letter to Hermann

Leon from Bad Arolsen has heard about the American boy who is looking for an exchange partner.
Write Leon's letter to Jason in your exercise book. Use the information below and ask at least one question.
Write about 120 words.

Leon Schießer

Age:
14, birthday in 2 months

Family:
father, mother, Lara (12) in a small house in Bad Arolsen

Hobbies:
football, swimming, doesn't play baseball, but there is a baseball club in the next city

Favourite subjects:
English, French, History

Berlin:
not been to Berlin, wants to go, interested in history too

Possible dates:
Jason: August – January in Germany, Leon: February – July in Hermann

___/18

SPEAKING

🎧 08 Calling your exchange partner

Listen to the telephone call between Moritz from Germany and his American exchange partner Mike.

👉 Höre dir Moritz Antworten an, unterbrich die Aufnahme und sprich sie abschnittsweise nach.
Falls du etwas nicht verstehst, höre den Abschnitt noch mal an. Wenn du mehr Hilfe benötigst, findest du den Hörtext im Lösungsheft.
Notiere hilfreiche Formulierungen aus den Antworten in Stichpunkten in dein Lernheft.
Deine Notizen helfen dir bei deinen eigenen Antworten in **Now you**.

🎧 09 Now you

Jason has written to your school too. Your family has invited him to stay with you from August until January next school year. He is calling to talk about the exchange.

___/20

Unit 3 | Klassenarbeit B 49

Unit 3 | Klassenarbeit B

MEDIATION

A day trip to Heidelberg

Your school is planning a day trip to Heidelberg. Your exchange student from the USA doesn't understand everything your teacher says.

10 **a)** *Listen to your teacher's announcements and explain them to your exchange student in English.* (3P)

Your teacher Wir treffen uns hier vor der Schule, der Bus fährt um Punkt 7 Uhr ab. Da wir mindestens zwei Stunden bis Heidelberg benötigen, können wir nicht warten, falls sich jemand verspätet. Also, bitte unbedingt den Wecker stellen.

Student I didn't get all the details about tomorrow. Do we have to bring an alarm clock[1]?

You No, you don't need to bring _____. But it's important that you _____ arrive _____.

11 **b)** *Now listen to more of your teacher's announcements. Help your friend in English.* (11P)

> ☞ Höre die Ansagen des Lehrers nur einmal an.
> Unterbrich nach jedem Abschnitt die Aufnahme und versuche, deinem Austauschpartner die Ansagen des Lehrers zu vermitteln.
> Vergleiche abschließend deine gesamte Lösung mit der Musterlösung.
> Wiederhole die Aufgabe und ergänze deine Lösungen.

Your teacher …

Student I understood that we're going to visit Heidelberg Castle. That's great. But what was that about the camera? And do we have to write something?

You We should bring our cameras _____

We need a pen and some paper for _____

Your teacher …

Student What was that about three people? I didn't understand what the teacher said.

You In the afternoon we have free time in Heidelberg. We have to _____

Student And do we have to do anything special in our groups?

You No, we _____

Student And where do we meet after that?

You _____

Your teacher …

Student We'll be back by 6 pm. Is there anything else that's important for me to know?

You Yes, _____

---

[1] alarm clock [əˈlɑːmklɒk] *Wecker*

Klassenarbeit A

Unit 4

Gesamtpunktzahl _____ /50 Note _____

LISTENING

🔊12 CASA – Come and see Atlanta!

*You are going to hear an announcement about Atlanta by the CASA travel agency¹.
Read the task and then listen to the announcement.*

About CASA

a) *While listening to the announcement, tick (✓) the correct ending.*

1 CASA offers tours …
   - a) of Atlanta.
   - b) of Georgia.
   - c) of Georgia and Atlanta.
   - d) in large cities in the south-west.

2 CASA has a lot of experience because …
   - a) they organize tours every day.
   - b) they've been organizing tours for 15 years.
   - c) the guides live in Atlanta.
   - d) they love showing people around.

3 CASA tours are for …
   - a) families only.
   - b) business people only.
   - c) everybody.
   - d) groups only.

4 On the tours visitors …
   - a) can have drinks.
   - b) can ask the guides questions.
   - c) can use headphones.
   - d) have to speak English.

___ /6

¹ travel agency [ˈtrævl ˈeɪdʒənsi] *Reisebüro*

Unit 4 | Klassenarbeit A

5	People who book the History Tour …	a) see the city centre.
		b) only visit the King Center.
		c) see important places and visit the King Center.
		d) see "Old Atlanta".

6	Tour 21 …	a) is one of the longer tours.
		b) is the right tour if you want to visit CNN.
		c) can't be found on the website.
		d) isn't a good tour for families.

___/23

LANGUAGE

___/9

1 WORDS Martin Luther King

Here is some information about Martin Luther King and the King Center.
Find the missing words and fill them in.

1 Don't miss the chance to visit the King Center … your visit to Atlanta.
  _ _ _ _ _

2 The young Martin Luther King worked for a Baptist church as a … .
  _ _ _ _ _ _ _

3 At that time blacks didn't have the same rights as whites – there was … .
  _ _ _ _ _ _ _ _

4 Martin Luther King fought for … for black people.
  _ _ _ _ _ _ _

5 At that time African Americans and white Americans were kept … .
  _ _ _ _ _ _ _ _

6 In 1963 Martin Luther King became famous through the … on Washington.
  _ _ _ _ _

7 There he made his famous … .
  _ _ _ _ _ _

8 April 4th is the … of his death.
  _ _ _ _ _ _ _ _ _ _

Can you make a word with the letters from the blue boxes? If not, look at sentence 9.

9 Most people who go to the King Center are very ⬚⬚⬚⬚⬚⬚⬚⬚⬚ .

2 GRAMMAR A weekend in Atlanta

___/10

Present perfect

(+) Bejahte Aussagesätze	(−) Verneinte Aussagesätze
I/you/we/they + have + Partizip Perfekt (3. Form)	I/you/we/they + haven't + Partizip Perfekt (3. Form)
he/she/it + has + Partizip Perfekt (3. Form)	he/she/it + hasn't + Partizip Perfekt (3. Form)
I**'ve** already **packed** my suitcase.	I **haven't packed** my suitcase yet.
He **has** already **made** some breakfast.	He **hasn't made** breakfast yet.

a) *John and his friends want to organize a weekend in Atlanta. Look at their list. What have they already done? (✔) What haven't they done yet? (✘) Write the sentences. Use **already** and **yet**.* (6P)

Our Atlanta tour: to do list

1. John – visit official Atlanta website ✔
2. Tim and Sue – search for tours of Atlanta ✔
3. Tim – buy a map ✘
4. Sue and Sally – find out about train times ✘
5. Sally – look for cheap hotels ✔
6. Sally – phone a hotel ✘

1 John _____

2 _____

3 _____

4 _____

5 _____

6 _____

b) *Write down two things that you have already done this week and two things you haven't done yet. Use **already** and **yet**.* (4P)

_____

_____

_____

_____

Unit 4 | Klassenarbeit A

3 GRAMMAR At the CASA office

___ /4

Zeitpunkt: since	Zeitraum: for
We've grown our own vegetables **since the year 2008**.	We've grown strawberries **for three years** now.

Nimm zwei Farbstifte und unterstreiche in den Sprechblasen unten in einer Farbe Zeitangaben, die sich auf einen **Zeitpunkt** beziehen und in einer anderen Zeitangaben, die sich auf einen **Zeitraum** beziehen.

*Alice works for CASA. It's been a very busy day. Write Alice's sentences with the verbs in the **present perfect**. Use **since** or **for**.*

1 The office – be full of customers – we opened this morning

2 The other tour guides and I – work without a break – 8 o'clock this morning

3 Visitors – call about more than 12 tours – Monday

4 I – talk to three visitors – more than 30 minutes

5 I – not have time to read my e-mails 24 hours

1 *The office has been full of customers since we opened this morning.*

2 _____

3 _____

4 _____

5 _____

MEDIATION

At the CASA travel agency

👉
- Übersetze nicht wörtlich, sondern sinngemäß.
- Gib das Wesentliche wieder.
- Verwende kurze und einfache Sätze.
- Umschreibe unbekannte Wörter.

The Kurz family from Göttingen is on holiday in Georgia. Today they are at the CASA travel agency in Atlanta because they would like to get to know Atlanta on a tour around the city. Their son Niklas helps his parents because they don't speak much English. Imagine you are Niklas.

Frau Kurz Sagst du bitte der Dame, dass wir eine Tour für vier Personen mitmachen möchten.

Niklas _____ (1P)

Lady Let's see. We've got different tours to choose from. What exactly do you want to see?

Niklas _____ (2P)

Herr Kurz Na ja, auf jeden Fall die Innenstadt, finde ich.

Niklas _____ (1P)

Lady Then I can offer you our Tour 21. You'll see all the sights in downtown Atlanta, you'll visit CNN* and the World of Coca-Cola and the tour ends at Underground Atlanta*.

Niklas _____ (4P)

Frau Kurz Was ist denn Underground Atlanta?

Niklas _____ (1P)

Lady It's a large area below street level[1] with many shops, restaurants and cinemas. It's an ideal place to relax after the long day tour. You could also have dinner there.

Niklas _____ (4P)

Lady If you're staying in a hotel in Atlanta, we can pick you up there at 10.30 in the morning.

Niklas _____ (2P)

Herr Kurz Mir gefällt die Tour. Niklas, frag bitte noch, wo und wann die Tour beginnt.

Niklas _____ (2P)

Frau Kurz Das ist ja wunderbar. Frag bitte, wie viel es für vier Personen kostet.

Niklas _____ (1P)

Lady We have a special offer for families: it's $42 for the four of you.

Niklas _____ (2P)

Herr Kurz Dann buchen wir die Tour für morgen.

Niklas _____ (1P)

* Eigennamen musst du nicht ins Deutsche übertragen.
[1] below street level [brˈləʊ striːt ˈlevl] *hier: unter der Erde*

/21

Unit 4 | Klassenarbeit A

Unit 4 — Klassenarbeit B

Gesamtpunktzahl ohne Speaking ____ /69 Note ____

Gesamtpunktzahl mit Speaking ____ /85 Note ____

____ /15

READING

Take Your Child To Work Day (TYCTWD)

In two weeks' time it's "Take Your Child to Work Day" again all over the US. My daughter (9 years old) wants to come to my office. Who has any experience with TYCTWD? Is it a good thing? I'm not sure what I should do. Any comments welcome.

Anne | 36 | Oneonta | 8th April | 10.00

Last year we had about 45 kids, aged 6–13 at our company. They toured the building, learned about what we do and, more importantly, ways we have fun. We organized a lot of activities for them, for example interviewing people who work for us and meeting two of our bosses in the conference room. We had also thought up some games which were very successful. When they first met in the morning, we had a game to get to know each other. We had a word search with all the names of people working in our department[1], we had puzzles and lots of activities that kept them moving around the building. By the end of the day most of the kids said they wanted to work in our office once they grew up. It was a great success.

Sue | 51 | Iowa | 8th April | 11.02

One of the best days I spent while growing up was when I went to work with my dad for the first time on TYCTWD. I still remember every minute of the day. I felt very grown up, as if I was already going to work. Of course I had a day off school so that was another good thing! But being together with my dad at his office and being able to watch him at work was a great experience for me. He took me along to a few meetings, we had lunch together in the cafeteria, and I helped him with a few things like taking messages to the secretary, making photocopies and things like that. The day motivated me to work harder at school. I can only say: it's a good thing! Once I have children of my own, I'll take them to my company on TYCTWD. Sure!

Terry | 25 | Philadelphia | 10th April | 9.00

The idea of TYCTWD is to show your children what you do at work. This day will also help your child to discover the link between what they learn at school and what they can do as a grown up. In most companies there are special hands-on activities for your child to do and workshops that will show him or her what your company does.

Before you take your daughter to your office you should make sure that:
– she is old enough to understand what you and your company are doing,
– the company offers special activities and workshops for her and the other kids,
– she doesn't miss too many important lessons at school,
– she is interested in what you do.

If you answer these questions with yes, then let her go to the office with you for the day!

Leona | 49 | Atlanta | 12th April | 4.36

---

[1] department [dɪˈpɑːtmənt] *Abteilung*

About the web discussion

Read the discussion in the web community and answer the questions in 1–5 words.

1 When and where does TYCTWD take place?

2 What do the students do on that day?

3 Where does Anne work?

4 What activities could the students take part in at Sue's company? (*three things*)

5 What did Terry do on his TYCTWD? (*three things*)

6 What should parents think about before their children take part in TYCTWD? (*three things*)

____ / 39

LANGUAGE

1 WORDS TYCTWD at CNN

a) *Last week a group of children spent a day at CNN together with their mum or dad. In the afternoon they made their own TV programme. Complete the table with the correct TV words.* (6P)

Time	2.00 pm	2.30 pm	3.00 pm	3.30 pm	4.00 pm	4.30 pm	5.00 pm
Title		Georgia's best school team: finals	Big brother	The price is right	True blood	Georgia news	CSI Miami
Programme	Love your pets						drama series

b) *Add four more words that have to do with TV or TV films. Find at least one verb.* (4P)

(to) be on, _____

c) *Write three sentences with the words.* (6P)

____ / 16

Unit 4 | Klassenarbeit B 57

Unit 4 | Klassenarbeit B

2 WORDS Jenny at her mum's office ___/7

Fill in the missing words. Choose from the box. Be careful: there are two more words than you need.

> disappointed • exact • freedom • immediately • impressed
> journalist • last • search engine • valuable

Last week Jenny and her mum went to work together. It was TYCTWD. Jenny's mum is a _____. Jenny was very _____ when she saw the big building her mum works in. As soon as they opened the door of her mum's office, she _____ started the computer. Her mum told her to look for some pictures for her next article. So Jenny entered some key words in the _____ of a picture database. TYCTWD was a _____ experience for Jenny. Jenny liked the work so much that she wished the day would _____ forever. Jenny was _____ that she couldn't join her mum the next day too.

3 GRAMMAR TYCTWD at AUM Technology ___/8

*AUM is a technology company with about 200 workers. Here is a text about their TYCTWD. Complete the sentences with the **present perfect**. Use **since** or **for**.*

1 They _____ (offer) TYCTWD _____ more than ten years now.

2 At the start only a few kids visited the company. But _____ 2002 this _____ (change). In that year the company started to offer special activities for the kids.

3 _____ the last five years the working parents _____ (always prepare) something special.

4 _____ 2010 they _____ (even ask) some newspaper reporters to come and report on the event.

4 GRAMMAR This year's TYCTWD

☞ **Simple past: active and passive**

Active ▶ Wer tut was?	**Passive** ▶ Mit wem geschieht etwas?
Bildung: 2. Form des Verbs (-ed/unregelmäßig)	Bildung: was/were + past participle (3. Form des Verbs)
They **drew** nice pictures.	Nice pictures **were drawn**.

_____/8

Fill in the correct forms of the verbs in the **simple past**. Be careful: some of them are **active**, others are **passive**.

1 At 7 o'clock the cleaners _____ (prepare) the room where the kids _____. (welcome)

2 Mrs Sutterland _____ very nice and _____ some muffins. (be, make)

3 13 children _____ to take part in TYCTWD. (invite)

4 The kids _____ in the lobby for the boss. (wait)

5 Then they _____ in the cafeteria. (welcome)

6 This year's TYCTWD _____ with an orange juice for everybody. (begin)

WRITING

1 Your opinion of TYCTWD

You have searched the internet and read the discussion in the web community. Write your own entry in your exercise book. What do you think about TYCTWD? Write about 100 words.

Write about …
- who you are and where you're writing from, (2P)
- activities like TYCTWD which exist in Germany, (3P)
- your opinion of TYCTWD, (2P)
- whether you'd like to have TYCTWD in Germany or not – give two reasons, (4P)
- one idea for an activity students could do during their day at work. (3P)

End your text in a friendly way. (1P)

 _____/15

Unit 4 | Klassenarbeit B

SPEAKING

___/16

🎧 13 Eric's day at the restaurant

Lots of students in class 8 at a high school in Atlanta took part in TYCTWD. Today they're reporting about their day. Listen to Eric.

👉 Höre dir Erics Vortrag noch einmal an und notiere dir nützliche Redewendungen. Sie helfen dir, wenn du in **Now you** selbst über deine Arbeitserfahrungen sprichst.

Now you

Now report about your experience. Speak about some work experience[1] you did or a Girls'/Boys' Day you took part in. Choose a job from the pictures below or talk about your own job.

Speak about …
- where you went, (2P)
- when your day started and ended, (2P)
- what you saw and did during the day, (at least four things) (8P)
- your opinion about the day and the job. (4P)

cook

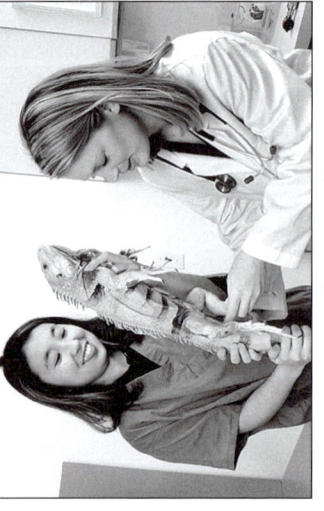
vet's assistant[3]

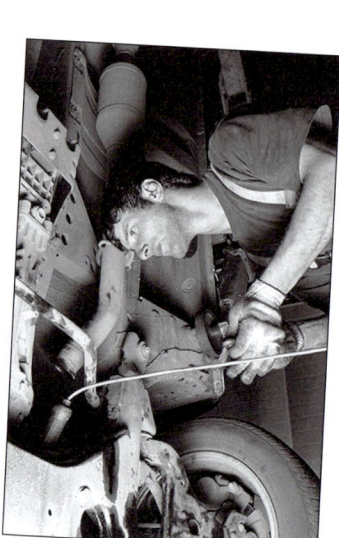
car mechanic[2]

make up artist

shop assistant

[1] work experience [wɜːk ɪkˈspɪəriəns] *Praktikum* [2] car mechanic [kɑː mɪˈkænɪk] *Kfz-Mechaniker/in*
[3] vet's assistant [vets əˈsɪstənt] *Tierarzthelfer/in*

Kompetenztest

Gesamtpunktzahl ohne Speaking _____ /71 Note _____

Gesamtpunktzahl mit Speaking _____ /86 Note _____

TEIL 1: LISTENING

Radio and TV in your lives – a radio programme

Listen to the radio programme about what British people like about radio and TV programmes. While you are listening, complete the table below. Tick the correct box or write 1 to 3 words if there is a question word. There is an example at the beginning (Emily). Listen to the recording only once. Take 20 seconds at the end of the recording to check your answers. Now take 30 seconds to look at the task.

	In the morning			During the day			In the evening		
	Radio	TV	Nothing	Radio	TV	Radio	TV
Emily			✓	When? *in the afternoon*	What?		What?
Steve	☐	☐	☐	When?	When?	What?	What?
Anne	☐	☐	☐	When?	When?	What?	What?

_____ /13

TEIL 2: SPEAKING

Me, my day, radio and TV

While you are staying in Southampton, England you are listening to the radio programme Teatime. The programme's presenter has asked listeners to tell him when they listen to the radio and when they watch TV during the day. He also wants to find out about listeners' favourite programmes.

Take ten minutes to prepare your call. Look at the pictures and the task. You can make notes.

Ring up and tell them ...
- who you are and where you are calling from.
- which programmes you listen to or watch in Germany ...
  – in the morning before you leave the house,
  – in the afternoon,
  – in the evening.

Give a reason why you listen to or watch one of the programmes.

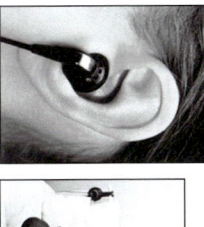

_____ /15

TEIL 3: MEDIATION ___/16

Your class is planning a school trip to the south-west of England. In groups you are preparing activities to do during your stay. You and your group are preparing a visit to Southwest Radio and TV, a local radio and TV station.

Read the information about tours at Southwest Radio and TV.

Southwest Radio and TV

A visit to the studios

Come and find out what goes on inside Southwest Radio and TV, your regional centre for radio and TV!
Your tour guide will give you an insight into our many programmes and he is ready to answer all your questions. Visitors will have the chance to see a real TV studio. You'll also pop into the radio studios and hear how radio programmes are produced.

You'll not only learn how television and radio programmes are made, you'll also have the chance to visit our interactive studio. Have a go at presenting the weather or be a star in your very own radio drama, complete with sound effects!

Southwest Radio and TV is a working building so no two tours are the same, but they will always be informative, interesting and fun.

Our tours

★ take about one hour and 45 minutes and involve a certain amount of walking and standing.
★ take place on Tuesdays at 10.00 am and 3.15 pm (plus Wednesdays and Saturdays from 14 July).
★ are open to anyone aged 10 years and over. A group tour booked for under-16s must have at least two accompanying adults.
★ take a maximum of 25 people on each tour.
★ have to be pre-booked.
★ are free of charge.

📷 You may take photos in the studios as advised by our tour guides, but some of the working areas are restricted. Video cameras are not permitted on the tours except in our Interactive Studio.

Contact us on 0044-1752-395953 or send an e-mail to visit@southwestradio.co.uk

Your classmates are asking you a lot of questions about the tour. Answer the questions in German. Use full sentences.

1 Ist es eine geführte Tour? Und was können wir bei der Führung alles sehen? (3 Dinge) (4P)

2 Kann man da auch selbst etwas machen und wenn ja, was? (2 Dinge) (2P)

3 Wie lange dauert die Tour?

4 Um wie viel Uhr beginnen die Touren?

5 Wie ist es mit der Gruppengröße?

6 Gibt es sonst Dinge, die wir als Schulklasse beachten müssen?

7 Darf man überall fotografieren und auch Videos drehen?

8 Muss man sich da anmelden und wie viel kostet der Besuch?

Kompetenztest

TEIL 4: READING

_____/12

The British and their soap operas

Read the text taken from a language magazine for students carefully. Then answer the questions below.

In Britain some of the most popular programmes on television are soap operas or soaps. Soaps are dramas usually shown in half hour episodes, three, four and sometimes five times a week. The most popular soaps in Britain are *Coronation Street* (known as *Corrie* by its fans) and *EastEnders*, although there are many more as well. Both *Coronation Street* and *EastEnders* have been running for a long time – in fact in December 2010 it was *Coronation Street's* 50th birthday. ITV, the TV channel which produces *Corrie*, showed a special live episode and a documentary about the history of the soap.

Coronation Street and *EastEnders* tell stories of the everyday lives of families living in Manchester and the East End of London. In both programmes community life often takes place in the local pub, the Rovers Return and the Queen Vic. As in other soap operas, stories with different characters are shown over many episodes, and there are always different stories running at the same time. Some of the characters have been in the shows for many years. The actors have become famous playing their roles, and the characters are loved by fans.

In British soaps the stories are unglamorous and show family life, friendship and conflicts. Over the years, *Coronation Street* and *EastEnders* have also included stories about difficult problems like AIDS, drugs, violence and alcoholism. In this way, soap operas have helped to change the way people think about important topics, although some stories have upset people. But not all the stories are so serious! There are also comedy storylines, which viewers like a lot too.

Soap operas play a very special role in British culture. Did you know that the very first British soap was made for the radio and is still being produced by the BBC today? The Archers started in 1951 and is still listened to by over 5 million people.

The very first TV soap operas were shown during the daytime and were mostly watched by housewives. The name soap opera comes from the fact that the programmes were often produced and supported by soap companies who wanted the viewers to buy their products, like washing powder. These days soaps in Britain are shown at prime time and have big audiences – both *Coronation Street* and *EastEnders* often have 10 million viewers.

Answer the questions. Write one to five key words only. Number 1 has been done for you as an example.

1 What are soap operas? *dramas, half hour episodes* _____

2 What are the most famous soaps on British TV? _____

3 Where do the characters in these soap operas live? _____

4 What are these soaps about? _____

5 Who watched the soaps when they first started? _____

6 What is the name of the first ever British soap? Can you watch it on television? _____

7 What did companies selling washing powder have to do with soap operas? _____

TEIL 5: WORDS

The British and their soap operas

___/12

a) *Find the word in the text for ...* (5P)

1 the different sections of a soap opera shown three, four or five times a week: _____

2 people who act in films, theatre or on television: _____

3 people who watch TV: _____

4 (to) make someone sad or angry: _____

b) *These words are from the text. Find one opposite for each word:*

1 many (line 4): _____

2 different (line 9): _____

3 serious (line 17): _____

4 daytime (line 22): _____

c) *Circle the word that doesn't fit in the group. There is an example at the beginning (1).*

1 often, sometimes, (never) usually

2 produce, sell, buy, watch

3 product, pub, company, shop

4 channel, film, programme, newspaper

5 soap, support, water, shower

TEIL 6: WRITING

An article for the school magazine

Your American friend is the editor of a school magazine. He has asked some students to write about their favourite films.

Write a short text of about 100 words about one of your favourite films.

Write about ...
- the name of the film and what it is about,
- when and where you saw it,
- the characters in the film,
- why you liked the film.

How to do well in a test

Countdown zum Testerfolg

Ein Test ist angekündigt? Kein Grund zur Panik. Wichtig ist, dass du weißt, worauf du dich vorbereiten musst. Im Zweifelsfall frag deine Lehrerin oder deinen Lehrer. Der Countdown kann beginnen!

Eine Woche vor dem Test

1 Lies noch einmal die **Texte** der zuletzt durchgenommenen Unit (A-Section und Text, eventuell auch das Background File). Fasse mündlich oder schriftlich zusammen, worum es ging.

2 Wiederhole den **Wortschatz** der Unit mit Hilfe des *Vocabulary* oder des *Wordmaster*. Schreibe dir die Wörter und Wortverbindungen, die du immer wieder vergisst, auf ein Blatt Papier. Eine Mindmap oder ein Wortfeld helfen beim Behalten.

3 Geh auch noch mal die neue **Grammatik** durch. Aufgaben zur Selbstüberprüfung und zum Üben findest du im *Practice*-Teil, auf der Seite „How am I doing?", im *Grammar File* (S. 160–171), in deinem *Workbook* und im *e-Workbook*.

Zwei Tage vor dem Test

1 Wiederhole den **Wortschatz**. Manche Wörter sitzen noch nicht? Schreibe einen kurzen Text, in dem du sie verwendest.

2 Lies die **Texte** ein weiteres Mal.

3 Erkläre einem Freund oder einer Freundin die neue **Grammatik**. Das klappt nicht richtig? Dann lies nochmal im *Grammar File* nach.

Am Abend vor dem Test

1 Entspanne dich. Du kannst lesen, dich in die Badewanne legen, Musik hören, fernsehen, …

2 Geh zur gewohnten Zeit ins Bett.

Am Morgen des Tests

1 Steh rechtzeitig auf, damit du nicht hetzen musst.

2 Lies irgendetwas „zum Aufwärmen", aber schau nicht mehr in dein Schülerbuch.

Während des Tests

1 Denk daran: Du hast dich gut vorbereitet. Es gibt keinen Grund, nervös zu sein.

2 Konzentriere dich auf den Test, lass dich nicht ablenken.

3 Lies dir die Aufgaben genau durch. Dann löse zuerst die Aufgaben, die dir einfach scheinen. Wende dich erst danach den schwereren Aufgaben zu.

4 Aufgaben, die du bearbeitet hast, hakst du ab. So siehst du, wie du vorankommst, und behältst den Überblick.

5 Schau ab und zu auf die Uhr. Du solltest dir für den Schluss noch etwas Zeit einplanen, um deine Antworten noch einmal durchzulesen und wenn nötig zu korrigieren.

Exam Skills

Aufgabenstellungen verstehen

Bevor du anfängst, die Aufgaben zu bearbeiten, vergewissere dich, dass du genau weißt, was du tun sollst. Lies die Aufgabe Wort für Wort langsam und gründlich und von Anfang bis Ende durch. Du kannst besonders wichtige Teile der Aufgabenstellung unterstreichen und die Aufgabe, wenn nötig, für dich in einzelne Schritte unterteilen.

Den folgenden Arbeitsanweisungen begegnest du häufig:

Add Verbinde eine Information oder einen Sachverhalt mit einer/einem anderen auf die geforderte Art und Weise.

Choose Wähle zwischen verschiedenen Möglichkeiten die passende Information aus.

Comment Kommentiere einen Sachverhalt durch die Darstellung deiner eigenen Meinung dazu. Begründe und erläutere sie möglichst genau.

Compare Vergleiche Dinge, Wörter oder Sachverhalte, indem du prüfst, ob und auf welche Weise sie gleiche oder verschiedene Eigenschaften, Aussehen, Bedeutungen oder Funktionen haben.

Complete Ergänze eine Information, indem du sie an dem dafür vorgesehenen Platz einträgst und damit z. B. einen Satz sinnvoll beendest.

Describe Beschreibe ein Objekt oder eine Person, d.h. stelle dar, wie sie aussehen, wie das Objekt funktioniert oder die Personen handeln. Vermeide eigene Wertungen wie z. B. „beautiful", „useful" oder „great".

Discuss Diskutiere ein Thema, eine Behauptung oder eine Aussage. Untersuche möglichst viele Seiten davon, z. B. Vor- und Nachteile, und stelle diese geordnet dar.

Explain Erkläre einen Sachverhalt, d. h. gib wesentliche Fakten über ihn und erläutere, wie sie logisch zusammenhängen.

Fill in Trage die geforderten Informationen in den dafür vorgesehenen Platz ein, z. B. in eine Lücke oder eine Tabelle.

List Schreibe einzelne oder mehrere Informationen übersichtlich und geordnet auf, z. B. in einer Reihe, Tabelle oder einem anderen Verzeichnis.

Listen Höre dir einen Text, einzelne Informationen oder Sachverhalte an.

Match Ordne die angegebenen Informationen einander zu, wie es die Aufgabe erfordert. Finde z. B. Satzanfänge und passende Satzenden und füge sie zusammen.

Use Verwende eine Tatsache, ein Wort usw. so, wie es in der Aufgabe gefordert wird.

Write a … Schreibe etwas in einem geforderten Textformat auf, z. B. deinen Kommentar zu etwas oder eine Geschichte.

English G 21

Klassenarbeitstrainer
für Schülerinnen und Schüler

Lösungen und Lerntipps

D4 Erweiterte Ausgabe

Cornelsen

Introduction

READING

Become a Junior Ranger!

1 About the text

– what a Junior Ranger is

– how to become a Junior Ranger

2 Junior Rangers and the Grand Canyon

	Right	Wrong	Not in the text
1 Junior Rangers learn about the Grand Canyon.	✓		
2 Children have to pay to go on a Junior Ranger programme.		✓	
3 The Rangers' programmes take place once a week.		✓	
4 Junior Rangers must be at least 4 years old.	✓		
5 If you are 6 years old, you can become a Raven Junior Ranger.	✓		
6 Junior Rangers can visit the Grand Canyon for free.			
7 Every Junior Ranger gets a baseball cap.		✓	
8 Phantom Ranch is open 365 days a year.			✓

LANGUAGE

1 WORDS An alphabetical list

a)

A	raeeudntv	adventure	N	eaivtN nrmAacie	Native American
B			O		
C	mteomcn	comment	P	orlpte osnttia	petrol station
D	iaydl	daily	Q		
E			R		
F	ieogfvr	forgive	S	lsea	sale
G	erdga	grade	T	olto	tool
H	whghyai	highway	U		
I			V		
J			W	gnwi	wing
K			X		
L	eesnlci ealtp	license plate	Y		
M	uoemmnnt	monument	Z	eonz	zone

b) Mögliche Lösungen:

middle school, gas, deep, grass, rim, awesome, three and a half, tip, tent, foot, natural, route, raise money, look forward to sth, hometown.

| **Lerntipp** | So kannst du **Wörter wiederholen** |

Die A-Z-Liste ist eine Möglichkeit, Wörter zu wiederholen.
- Trage bei jedem Buchstaben ein neues Wort ein.
- Überprüfe die Vollständigkeit und die Rechtschreibung mit deinem Schülerbuch.
- Trage fehlende oder falsch geschriebene Wörter mit einer besonderen Farbe ein und lerne sie gezielt.
- Schreibe die deutsche Bedeutung zu den Wörtern oder erkläre sie auf Englisch.

2 Getting by in English

1 I have no idea where to go.
2 Can you tell me how to get to the station, please?
3 I have no idea what to do.
4 I have no idea who to ask.

| **Lerntipp** | So kannst du **Getting by in English** üben |

Wenn du die Vokabeln zur Unit lernst, solltest du unbedingt die ganz rechte Spalte im Vocabulary-Teil deines Schülerbuchs mitlernen. Hier siehst du, wie die neuen Wörter in ganzen Sätzen angewendet werden.

3 GRAMMAR Talking about national parks

1 I went to the Grand Canyon with my family last summer.
2 I haven't hiked in the Grand Canyon yet.
3 Last week I gave a presentation on national parks in the US.
4 I didn't have time yesterday to tell you about my trip to Death Valley.
5 We have visited many national parks in the past few years, but we haven't been to the Grand Canyon yet.

| **Lerntipp** | **Simple past** oder **present perfect**? |

Lies dir noch einmal die Signalwörter im Hinweis zu der Aufgabe durch und unterstreiche sie dann in den Sätzen.
Bilde ähnliche Sätze mit diesen Signalwörtern. Schreibe sie in dein Lernheft.

Introduction

4 GRAMMAR Junior Rangers on the internet

a)

1 What does a Park Ranger do to protect the park?
2 Why did you become a Junior Ranger? / Why did you want to become a Junior Ranger? / Why did you decide to become a Junior Ranger?
3 Was the programme with the Park Ranger interesting?
4 How did you hear about the Junior Ranger programme?
5 What did you do to become a Junior Ranger? / What did you have to do to become a Junior Ranger? / What do you have to do to become a Junior Ranger?
6 Where did you find out about the Junior Ranger programme?

Now you

b)

Mögliche Lösungen:

1 When did you become a Junior Ranger?
2 Was it free to become a Junior Ranger?
3 Are there any other Junior Ranger programmes?
4 When did you visit the Grand Canyon? / When did you go to the Grand Canyon?

Lerntipp Wiederholung der Zeiten

Falls du noch unsicher mit der Zeitenbildung bist, findest du hier einen Überblick:

Simple present	I walk	I go	I do
Present progressive	I am walking	I am going	I am doing
Simple past	I walked	I went	I did
Past progressive	I was walking	I was going	I was doing
Present perfect	I have walked	I have gone	I have done
Past perfect	I had walked	I had gone	I had done
Will-future	I will walk	I will go	I will do

Bilde die entsprechenden Zeiten von **drei weiteren Verben** und schreibe sie in dein Lernheft. Mindestens eins davon sollte ein unregelmäßiges Verb sein.

STUDY SKILLS

PARAPHRASING Andy explains

Mögliche Lösungen:

1 A Park Ranger is a person who works in a National Park. They look after the park.
2 We sell baseball caps at the Grand Canyon. A baseball cap is something that you wear on your head. It protects you from the sun.
3 You can stay in a tent at the Grand Canyon. A tent is something you can sleep in outside.
4 There are bears at the Grand Canyon. A bear is an animal that is large, brown or black, dangerous and lives in woods.

WRITING
An article about the Grand Canyon

a)

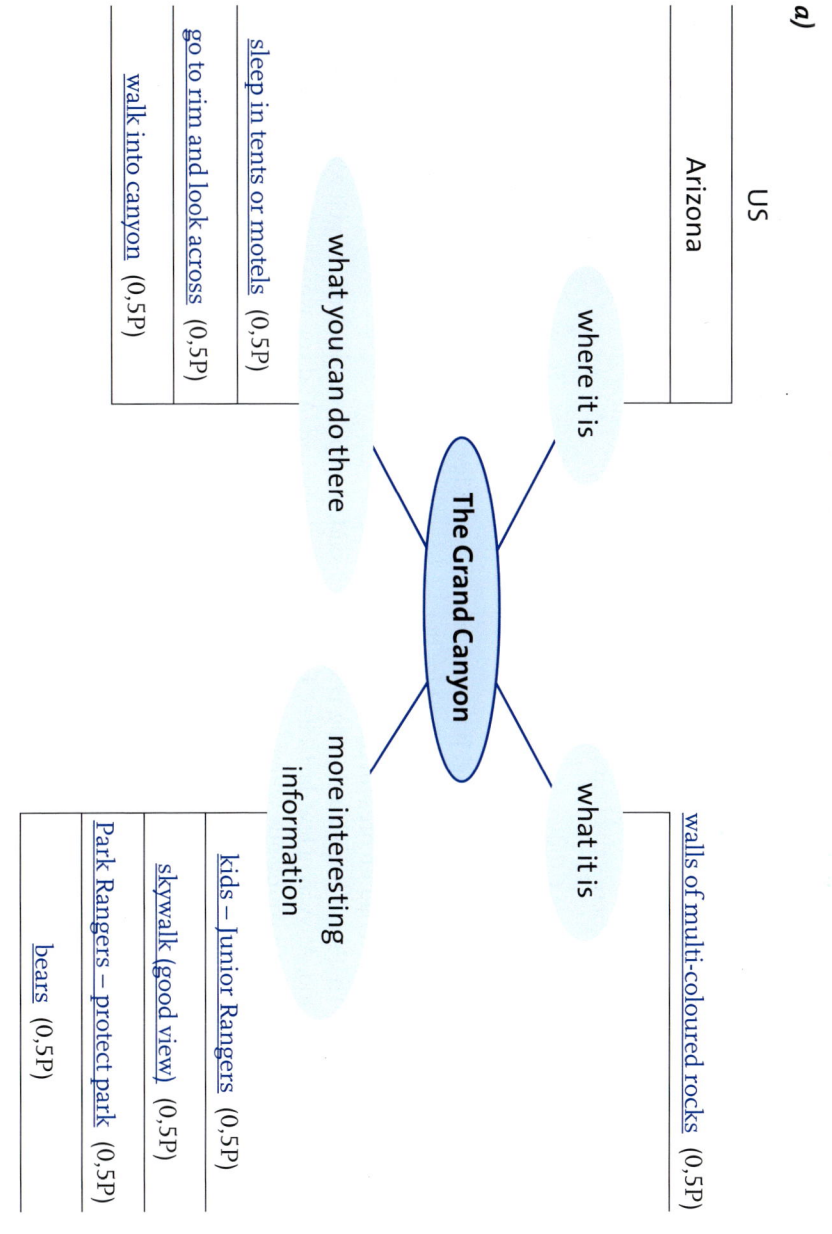

b)

Mögliche Lösung:

About the Grand Canyon

The Grand Canyon is in the US, in the state of Arizona. It's an amazing national park with walls of multi-coloured rocks. (2P)

There are many interesting things to do in the Grand Canyon. (2P) First, you should go to the skywalk, because from there you have a brilliant view. (2P) You can go on long hikes and walk down into the Canyon or you can use your car for day trips. (2P) You might even see a bear. (2P)

There are beautiful motels where you can sleep. (2P) If you like, you can also stay in a tent. (2P) Park Rangers look after the park and the animals. (2P) It's their job to protect the park and the visitors in the park. (2P) Kids can become Junior Rangers too and help to protect the park. (2P)

Unit 1

LISTENING

🎧 01 Big Apple Radio

Radio presenter	Good afternoon everybody. I'm Lucy Knight and you're listening to BAR – Big Apple Radio. Welcome to our program "Life in New York". Today we're talking about the subway. We're asking you, our listeners, to tell us your personal stories about the subway. Phone now with your story … … And here's my first call. Big Apple Radio, hello?
Cindy	Hello, I'm Cindy.
Radio presenter	Hello, Cindy. Thanks for calling. Now, before you start with your story tell us when it happened.
Cindy	Well, it was last spring. It was my friend's birthday, so I took the subway to see her. I was so proud of my present for her – a beautiful book about Australia. I was a bit late and had to hurry. And then something terrible happened – I left the present on the subway.
Radio presenter	So you had no present for your friend!
Cindy	That's it. I was so unhappy, because as I said, the book was very nice and it was expensive too. Anyway, a few days later, I got this telephone call. And you won't believe it – it was from a young guy who had found the book. I always write something nice in a book before I give it as a present – a poem or just a nice sentence – and then I add the date, my name and my telephone number.
Radio presenter	You were very lucky …
Cindy	True. The guy phoned me and even came to my apartment with the book – and we've become friends. We still see each other at least once a month.
Radio presenter	What a happy ending. Thank you very much, Cindy. After some more music we'll hear from another listener.
Sam	Hi, this is Sam.
Radio presenter	Hi, Sam. Thanks for your call. Now Sam, you are one of our young listeners. … How old are you?
Sam	I'm twelve.
Radio presenter	And you have a story to tell us about the subway, Sam, don't you?
Sam	Yes, you see, last Sunday my brother and I wanted to use the subway. But when we were standing in front of the ticket machine at the subway station, I realized that I didn't have enough money for the two of us. The tickets were $2.25 each but I only had $3.50, so $1 was missing. We must have looked quite unhappy because a woman asked us what the problem was. And a second later we had enough money for our ride on the subway. So I want to say thank you to the nice woman who helped us last Sunday. I'm sorry I don't know your name but I hope you're listening.
Radio presenter	Another good story. Thanks, Sam. If you want to tell us … Oh, here's our next call, Big Apple Radio, hello?
Ana-María	Hello, this is Ana-María from Spain. I've just heard Sam's story. I'm here on vacation and everybody on the subway is so friendly. You see, I didn't know anything about the subway when I came here. But there has never been a problem: people help you to find the right station, they tell you where and how to get tickets, once you're on the subway they tell you where to get off and how to find the place you want to go. It's great.
Radio presenter	Thank you, Ana-María. And have a great time here in New York, the city that never sleeps. Thanks again for all your interesting stories. We'll continue after some music.

1 Subway stories

B, E, D

2 About the radio programme

	The presenter	Cindy	Sam	Ana-Maria
1 This person is talking about something that happened last spring.		✓		
2 This person is talking about something that happened last weekend.			✓	
3 This person was in a hurry.		✓		
4 This person made a friend.		✓		
5 This person has met lots of nice people on the subway.				✓
6 This person couldn't pay for his/her subway ticket.			✓	
7 This person works in the afternoon.			✓	
8 This person wants to say "thank you".				✓
9 This person thinks that people in New York are friendly.				✓

LANGUAGE

1 WORDS The five boroughs of New York

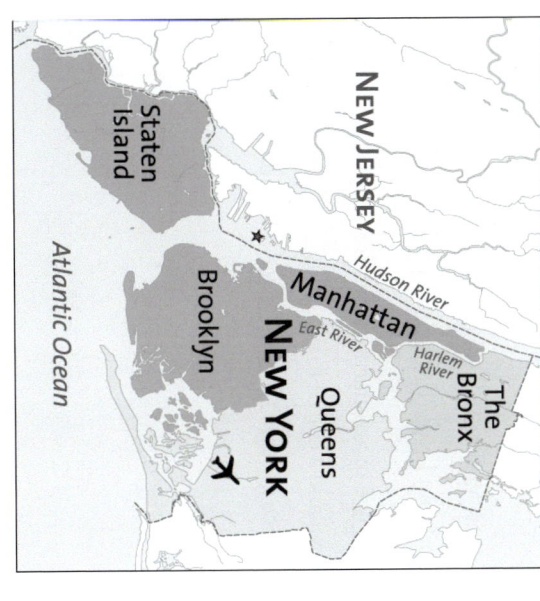

Mögliche Lösungen (zwei davon):

the Bronx — in the north, not an island
Manhattan — an island between the Hudson River and East River, with many skyscrapers
Queens — largest borough, in the south-west of Long Island
Brooklyn — on Long Island, the famous Brooklyn Bridge links Brooklyn and Manhattan
Staten Island — an island near New York Harbor, ferry from here to Manhattan

Unit 1 | Lösungen A

2 WORDS At the museum

1 Admission to the museum is $8.
2 Let's get our tickets at the ticket office over there.
3 The museum has a large collection of dinosaurs.
4 The museum is often very crowded.
5 A special workshop for children takes place every Sunday.
6 You can walk or stand on it.   sidewalk

3 GRAMMAR Life in the city

1 I like taking photos of all the cool buildings here.
2 I love visiting the museums.
3 My sister and I don't like going by subway.
4 Riding a bike can be dangerous in New York.
5 I dream of living in Brooklyn some day.
6 Shopping is great in New York. Here you can shop till you drop!

Now you

Mögliche Lösungen:
I love sitting in the park.
I don't like waiting in lines/queues.
Going to the movies/cinema is great.

4 GRAMMAR My life in New York

1 If I go to New York next summer, I will/'ll watch the New York Yankees play football. I will/'ll eat lots of hamburgers and fries. I will not/won't do much sport, but I will/'ll watch a lot of television.

2 If I lived in New York, I wouldn't live on my own. I would/'d live in an apartment with friends. I would/'d go to the deli every day and I would/'d buy a bagel and a coffee to go. I would/'d go everywhere by subway or bus. I would/'d run in Central Park once or twice a week. I would/'d see a Broadway show once a month.

WRITING

A subway story for the school magazine

Mögliche Lösung:

Lost and found (1P)

It was last week and I was on the subway after school. (2P) Most days I have to stand on the subway, but that day I was lucky and was able to sit down. (2P) A man with a parcel sat opposite me. (1P) When he stood up to leave, he left his parcel. (2P) I saw what had happened and I called, "You've forgotten your parcel". (2P) But he didn't hear me and got off the train. (1P)

What could I do? (1P) I saw that there was a name and a telephone number on the parcel, so I phoned the number. (2P) I spoke to the man and 30 minutes later he was at my door. (2P) When I gave him the parcel, he was very happy. (2P) He didn't only say "thank you" – he gave me some money: I got $50! (2P)

| **Lerntipp** | **Korrigieren und Verbessern** |

Nach dem Schreiben eines Textes solltest du immer noch genügend Zeit für die Überarbeitung deines Textes einplanen.

- Überprüfe zunächst, ob du alle Hinweise aus der Aufgabenstellung beachtet hast und korrigiere deinen Text gegebenenfalls.
- Unterstreiche alle Verbformen und überlege, ob du **simple past** verwendet hast und ob die Formen richtig sind. Nutze dabei Hilfen aus dem Schülerbuch (z.B. von der Liste mit den unregelmäßigen Verben auf S. 258).
- Wenn verneinte Sätze und Fragen in deinem Text vorkommen, solltest du noch mal genau überlegen, ob sie richtig gebildet sind.

Unit 1 Lösungen B

READING

The Empire State Building Run-Up

1 What is the article about?

a) the history of the Empire State Building.
b) a race up the stairs of the Empire State Building. ✓
c) visiting the Empire State Building.
d) fire safety in the Empire State Building.

2 Missing headings

1	2	3	4
B	F	D	A

3 About the Run-Up

1 e The Empire State Building Run-Up <u>takes place every year.</u>
2 h People who would like to run <u>have to write a letter to the New York Road Runners Club.</u>
3 f The Run-Up was the idea of <u>the President of the New York Road Runners Club.</u>
4 a About 500 runners <u>want to be in the race.</u>
5 d It is a hard race, so <u>runners must be really fit.</u>

Now you

Mögliche Lösungen:

1 Fred Lebow wanted more people <u>to run / to get interested in running.</u>
2 Not everyone can <u>run in the race.</u>
3 A student has won <u>the race four times.</u>

Lerntipp Completing sentences

Bei dieser Art von Aufgabe musst du auf zwei unterschiedliche Dinge achten:

1. Der Inhalt deines zusammengesetzten Satzes muss mit den Informationen aus dem Text übereinstimmen.
2. Dein zusammengesetzter Satz muss grammatikalisch richtig sein.

Nur wenn du auf beide Punkte geachtet hast, ist deine Antwort richtig.

4 Questions about the Run-Up

1. When is the next race?
2. How many floors do the runners run up?
3. When was the first race?
4. What are the prizes for the winners?
5. How do the runners train for the race?
6. Are there stair races in other parts of the world?
7. How many people run in the race?
8. How old do you have to be to run in the race?
9. Are the runners only from New York?
10. Is there a women's race?
11. Can I watch the race?
12. Have there been any accidents?

LANGUAGE

1 WORDS American and British English

a) *Mögliche Lösungen:*

American English	British English
cellphone	mobile (phone)
line	queue
downtown	city centre
elevator	lift
gas	petrol
grade	year
sidewalk	pavement

b) *Mögliche Lösungen:*

American English	British English
center	centre
meter	metre
theater	theatre
color	colour
favorite	favourite
harbor	harbour
neighbor	neighbour

Unit 1 | Lösungen B   11

Unit 1 | Lösungen B

2 WORDS In the US

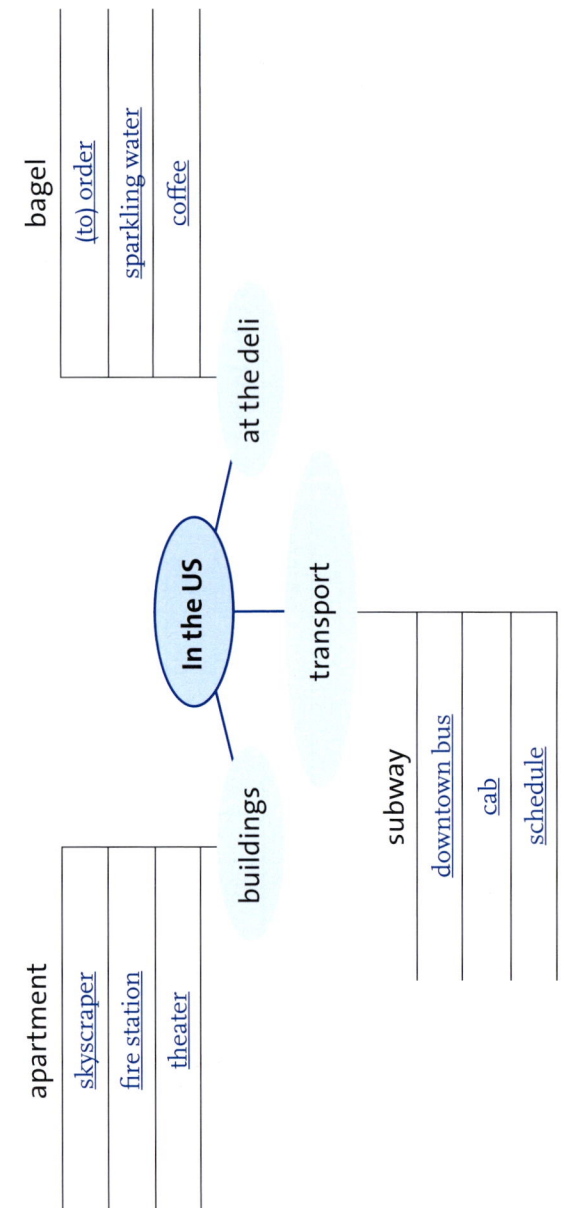

3 GRAMMAR About sport

2 Mike dreams of playing football in a big stadium.
3 Alice is thinking of playing volleyball.
4 Mark is not/isn't good at swimming.
5 Elly is interested in doing yoga.
6 Alan is good at running.

Now you

Mögliche Lösungen:
I'm not interested in playing football.
I'm good at running.
I dream of playing tennis at Wimbledon.

MEDIATION

Visiting New York City

1 Informationen über die Aussichtsplattform im 86. Stockwerk (5 *davon*)
- 320 Meter hoch
- schnelle, automatische Aufzüge
- zwei Bereiche: verglaster Innenbereich, der im Winter beheizt und im Sommer gekühlt wird
- großer Außenbereich an allen vier Seiten des Gebäudes
- es gibt starke Ferngläser (für eine geringe Gebühr)
- behinderte Besucher sind willkommen

2 Informationen über die Eintrittskarten für die Aussichtsplattform im 102. Stockwerk
Man muss sie unten bei Ankunft kaufen, (1P) sie kosten $ 15 zusätzlich zur normalen Eintrittskarte. (1P)

3 Öffnungszeiten der Aussichtsplattformen
Die Aussichtsplattformen sind jeden Tag offen. (1P) Sie sind bis 2 Uhr morgens geöffnet, (1P) man muss beachten, dass der letzte Aufzug nach oben um 1.15 Uhr fährt. (1P)

4 Informationen über den „Empire State Building Express Pass"
Der Empire State Building Express Pass kostet $ 45. (1P) Er wurde eingeführt, weil die Leute sagten, sie hätten keine Zeit die Aussichtsplattformen zu besuchen, weil man da so lange anstehen muss. (2P) Der Vorteil ist: Man kann bei jeder der drei Warteschlangen immer nach vorne gehen. (1P)

5 Gibt es einen Vorteil, wenn man bereits eine Eintrittskarte hat?
Man braucht dann nur in zwei der drei Schlangen zu warten. (1P)

Lerntipp | Mediation

- Sieh dir immer die Aufgabenstellung an, bevor du mit dem Lesen des Textes beginnst. Das spart Zeit bei der Beantwortung der Aufgaben.
- Markiere dir beim Lesen gleich wichtige Informationen, die du zur Lösung benötigst.
- Du kannst Mediation mit jedem englischen (oder deutschen) Text üben, indem du ihn liest und dann den Inhalt kurz auf Deutsch (bzw. auf Englisch) zusammenfasst.

Im Skills File auf S. 152 in deinem Schülerbuch findest du noch weitere Hilfen zum Thema Mediation.

Unit 1 | Lösungen B

SPEAKING

🎧 02 A street interview

Interviewer	Hello, can I ask you a few questions?
Spanish visitor	Yes, of course.
Interviewer	Can you tell me a bit about yourself?
Spanish visitor	Well, I'm from Valencia in Spain and I'm 26 years old.
Interviewer	Are you here on vacation or on business?
Spanish visitor	I'm here on business.
Interviewer	Where are you staying in New York City? And how long are you staying for?
Spanish visitor	I'm staying in a hotel in Queens. I'm here for four days.
Interviewer	Are you here on your own?
Spanish visitor	Yes, that's right.
Interviewer	How long have you been here and what have you seen?
Spanish visitor	I've been here for two days. I haven't seen very much because I've been working, but yesterday I went to the Bronx Zoo and was in Chinatown.
Interviewer	What kind of transport have you used here in New York?
Spanish visitor	I've travelled by subway and by cab. Cabs are a quick and good way to see the city.
Interviewer	So what do you like about New York?
Spanish visitor	I like eating in the many restaurants here. The food's great! Going to Chinatown was really interesting too!
Interviewer	Is there anything that you don't like?
Spanish visitor	Well, I don't like having to walk. Some streets here are very long, so then I take a cab.
Interviewer	Will you come to New York again?
Spanish visitor	Yes, there's so much to see. I'd love to come here again, but next time I won't be working!
Interviewer	Thanks for your time. Have a nice day!

Now you

🔊 03

Mögliche Lösung:

Interviewer	Hello, can I ask you a few questions?
You	Yes, of course. (1P)
Interviewer	Can you tell me a bit about yourself?
You	I'm from … in Germany and I'm … years old. (2P)
Interviewer	Are you here on vacation or on business?
You	I'm here on vacation. (1P)
Interviewer	Where are you staying in New York City? And how long are you staying for?
You	I'm staying in a youth hostel in the Bronx. I'm here for a week. (2P)
Interviewer	Are you here on your own?
You	No, I'm here with friends. (1P)
Interviewer	How long have you been here and what have you seen?
You	I've been here for four days. I've been to Chinatown and I've seen the Statue of Liberty. (3P)
Interviewer	What kind of transport have you used here in New York?
You	I've travelled by subway and by bus. The subway is really good: very clean and fast. (4P)
Interviewer	So what do you like about New York?
You	I like visiting all the sights. There's so much to see here! (2P)
Interviewer	Is there anything that you don't like?
You	Yes, I don't like taking the subway when it's busy! (2P)
Interviewer	Will you come to New York again?
You	Yes, I will. I want to visit all the museums and see a show on Broadway. (2P)
Interviewer	Thanks for your time. Have a nice day!

Unit 2

Lösungen A

LISTENING

🎧 04 Which is the best school trip – Yosemite National Park or San Diego?

Mrs Astbury OK, listen up everyone. Last week some students gave a presentation on Yosemite National Park. They showed us some exciting places to go and they presented a lot of activities the class could do during our trip in the summer. Today it's the second group's turn. They're going to tell us some interesting things about a possible trip to the city of San Diego. So, please, listen carefully.
And now over to you, John.

John Thank you. OK, Sue, Lucy, Tom and I have found out some interesting facts about San Diego. We're sure that our short presentation will help you to decide where we should go – and we hope it will be San Diego.

Lucy So, let's start with the journey. On this map you can see that it's not too far to San Diego. If we start early in the morning, say at about 6 am, we'll arrive at our hostel in San Diego at lunchtime. After a quick lunch we could start with a city tour, you know – to get a first impression. Just have a look at these photos of San Diego. We haven't worked out every detail of the plan for the city tour yet – that's one of the jobs that we'll do as soon as we know if we're going to San Diego.

Sue There'll be two main activities on our second day: in the morning we want to visit the famous San Diego Zoo. There are more than 4,000 animals in the zoo!
...
OK, OK, we know you've all been to a zoo already. That's why we've planned a special guided tour. It's a kind of quiz tour – you know, a tour where we have to find out things and so we'll get to know a special part of the zoo really well. We would have to ask the zoo for more information and about getting a special group price. That's the second job that we will do.

Tom As we'll have worked hard in the morning, we thought we could relax in the afternoon and go to the famous San Diego Ocean Beach. Just have a look at this amazing photo! We can lie in the sun, go swimming or even try to learn surfing. We could talk to a surf school about lessons – that's another job that we will have to do!
...

Lucy There are two ideas for our last day: a visit to San Diego harbor with a one-hour boat tour, or we could book one of the famous San Diego ghost tours!
...

John Thank you, Lucy. Now, are there any questions or comments on our San Diego school trip?
Student What about the evenings? Do you have any ideas for the evenings?
John Well, we have a lot of different ideas but we haven't worked out anything special yet – it's another job for us to do as soon as we know if we're going to San Diego.

Mrs Astbury So, thank you to your group, you've done well. Now everyone, please think about where you'd like to go: Yosemite National Park or San Diego. We'll talk about our school trip again next Tuesday and then you'll have to decide.

1 The San Diego presentation

E, D, B, A

2 Who in the class?

		✓
1 The first group …	a) has already given a presentation.	✓
	b) thinks Yosemite National Park is boring.	
	c) has talked about a climbing tour.	
	d) wants to stay in a hostel.	
2 The teacher …	a) has visited Yosemite National Park.	
	b) talks about last week's presentation.	✓
	c) wants to go to San Diego.	
	d) doesn't like the second presentation.	
3 The second group …	a) wants to arrive in San Diego in the evening.	
	b) wants to go on a special guided tour.	✓
	c) wants to go to the beach on the last day of the trip.	
	d) wants to go on a 30-minute boat trip.	
4 The class …	a) thinks San Diego is too far.	
	b) has no questions about the San Diego trip.	
	c) can't decide.	
	d) has to decide on Tuesday.	✓

3 Things to do
(drei davon)

1 work out a plan for the city tour
2 ask for more information about the quiz tour and the price
3 talk to the surf school
4 work out a programme for the evenings

LANGUAGE

1 WORDS Questions about the trip to San Diego

1 Is San Diego close to the Pacific Ocean?
2 I know about the zoo but what other attractions are there in San Diego?
3 What is the population of San Diego? It's a big city, right?
4 Are there many homeless people in San Diego?
5 Are there any disadvantages of going to San Diego?
6 San Diego is in California. Who is the governor of California?
7 What products are made in San Diego?
8 Do you think that the people who want to go to San Diego are in the minority?

Unit 2 | Lösungen A 17

Unit 2 | Lösungen A

> **Lerntipp** Einfügen von Wörtern
>
> Sieh dir die Sätze, in die du die richtigen Wörter einfügen sollst, genau an. Kannst du darin Hinweise finden, die dir eventuell bei der Lösung helfen? Im Falle von den Artikeln (**a/an, the**) z.B. muss ein Substantiv folgen.

2 WORDS Who or what is it?

1 grapes
2 border
3 sportsman
4 gardener
5 vegetarian

3 GRAMMAR Facts about California

a)

1 A lot of films are made in Hollywood.
2 San Francisco is named after Francis of Assisi.
3 Even today gold is found in California.
4 Oranges are grown in California.
5 California is known for its endless beaches.
6 Universal Studios in Hollywood is visited by many tourists every year.

b)

Mögliche Lösungen:

1 My area is known for its famous church.
2 A lot of wine is made in my area.
3 Apples are grown in my area.

> **Lerntipp** Passivformen
>
> ■ Zur Bildung des Passivs benötigst du die 3. Form des Verbs (**past participle**). Diese Form findest du bei den unregelmäßigen Verben auf S. 258/59 in deinem Englischbuch.
>
> ■ Lerne die Verben und ihre Formen in überschaubaren „Paketen" zu je 8–10 Verben. Wenn du mit einem neuen „Verbenpaket" beginnst, wiederhole die zuvor gelernten Wörter noch einmal.

4 GRAMMAR The school trip

a)
1 Four students were chosen to present their ideas.
2 A lot of photos were shown to the class.
3 A map was drawn on the board.
4 Two different activities were spoken about for the last day of the trip.
5 The zoo tour was described well.
6 The class was/were asked to decide on the school trip later.

b)
Mögliche Lösungen:
1 Two students were chosen to present the topic to the class.
2 A poster was shown to the class.
3 The students were asked lots of questions about their topic.

MEDIATION
Come on our ghost tour!

Mögliche Lösungen:

1 Es ist eine Geistertour, auf der man verschiedene „Geister" trifft, die vor ein oder zwei Jahrhunderten in San Diego gelebt haben. (3P) Die Tour wird von einem „Geisterjäger" geführt. (1P) Das Besondere ist, dass er die Geister scheinbar nicht sieht, die Besucher aber schon. (2P) Die Tour findet freitags und samstags jeweils um 18:30 und um 19:00 Uhr abends statt. (2P) Sie kostet $ 10 pro Person. (1P) Man sollte 15 Minuten vor Beginn am Visitor Information Center sein. (2P)

2 Am ersten und zweiten Freitag im Monat gibt es Sonderpreise, die nur für Gruppen ab zwölf Personen gelten. (2P) Die Sonderpreise gelten nur für die Tour um 18:30 Uhr. (1P) Reservierungen können nur im Internet gemacht werden. (1P)

Lerntipp | Die Bedeutung von Wörtern oder Ausdrücken aus dem Zusammenhang entnehmen

■ Lies den letzten Abschnitt des Flyers noch einmal. Überlege, was die Bedeutung von **first-come-first-served basis** sein könnte.
■ Welche Wörter aus dem Begriff sind dir schon bekannt? Worum geht es in dem Text? Versuche auf diese Weise eine erste Idee über die mögliche Bedeutung des Ausdruckes zu gewinnen. Überlege nun, wie man die Bedeutung auf Deutsch am besten zum Ausdruck bringt (eine wortwörtliche Übertragung ist meistens nicht die beste Lösung).
■ Schreibe deinen Vorschlag in dein Lernheft (Lösung s. S. 20).
■ Übe die Übertragung ins Deutsche, wenn du solchen Ausdrücken begegnest, z.B. **park and ride, come and see, coffee to go, …**

Unit 2 | Lösungen A

Lösungen zu S. 19:

First come, first served – Wer zuerst kommt, mahlt zuerst.

Park and ride – Parken Sie Ihr Auto und fahren Sie mit öffentlichen Verkehrsmitteln weiter.

Come and see – Sieh und staune

Coffee to go – Kaffee zum Mitnehmen

SPEAKING

05 Getting information on the phone

Chris	Big Wave Surf Center, you're talking to Chris Wiseman. How can I help you?
Student	Hello, this is Lucy Hilton from Goldwater High School. We're coming to San Diego on a school trip and would like to come to your surf camp. That's why I'm calling.
Chris	OK. Do you have the dates of your trip?
Student	Yes. Our school trip will be from June 1st – 3rd.
Chris	And what would you like to know about the surf camp?
Student	What are your opening hours?
Chris	Hmm, June, that's when we have our summer opening hours. Our hours are from 9 am to 6 pm.
Student	Do you have special lessons at the surf camp for schools?
Chris	What grade are you in and how many people will be coming?
Student	I'm in grade 8. There are 17 of us, 15 teenagers and two adults.
Chris	Let me have a look. Well, we have our "teen surf" lesson where you will learn to stand and ride waves.
Student	That sounds really great. How much time would we need for the lesson?
Chris	Well, about three hours.
Student	What time do the lessons start?
Chris	Lessons are daily and start at 9 am and 1 pm.
Student	Thanks. And how much would a lesson cost?
Chris	Let me see. That would be $30 per person. Would you like to book the lesson now?
Student	No, I'll have to speak to my teacher and the class first. I'll call you again next week. Thank you very much for your help. Goodbye.
Chris	You're welcome. Goodbye.

🔊 06 Now you

Hinweis

Wenn du Schwierigkeiten hast, das Gespräch zu verstehen, hast du hier die Möglichkeit, die Fragen und Antworten der Sprecherin zu lesen. Decke in diesem Fall die *Mögliche Lösung* darunter noch ab.

1 *San Diego Zoo:* San Diego Zoo, you're talking to Susan Baker. How can I help you?
2 *San Diego Zoo:* OK. And do you have the dates of your trip?
3 *San Diego Zoo:* And what would you like to know about the zoo?
4 *San Diego Zoo:* Hmm, May 2nd – 5th, that's in our spring opening hours. Our hours are from 9 am to 6 pm.
5 *San Diego Zoo:* What grade are you in and how many people will be coming?
6 *San Diego Zoo:* Let me have a look. Well, we have a tour where you will learn lots of interesting facts about the zoo and its animals.
7 *San Diego Zoo:* Well, about 2 1/2 hours.
8 *San Diego Zoo:* The tour starts at 1 pm.
9 *San Diego Zoo:* Let me see. That would be $25 per person. Would you like to book the tour now?
10 *San Diego Zoo:* You're welcome. Goodbye.

Mögliche Lösung:

1 *You:* Hello, this is John Stacey from Kennedy High School. We're coming to San Diego on a school trip and would like to visit your zoo. That's why I'm phoning.
2 *You:* Yes. Our school trip will be from May 2nd – 5th.
3 *You:* What are your opening hours?
4 *You:* Do you have a special tour of the zoo for schools?
5 *You:* I'm in grade 8. There are 30 of us, 28 teenagers and two adults.
6 *You:* That sounds really great. How much time would we need for the tour?
7 *You:* What time does the tour start?
8 *You:* Thanks. And how much would a tour cost?
9 *You:* No, I'll have to speak to my teacher and the class first. I'll call you again tomorrow. Thank you very much for your help. Goodbye.

Unit 2 — Lösungen B

READING

"Earthquakes: we want to be prepared"

1 Headings

Mögliche Lösungen (drei davon):

1. Why San Jose High School is taking part
2. The safety team and the plans
3. First steps / Earthquake bags
4. Special lessons about earthquakes / Activities
5. Join in too

2 FAQ

Mögliche Lösungen:

1. third Thursday in October
2. once a year
3. because it's in San Diego, California, earthquake country
4. parents, students and teachers
5. work out programme for ESD
6. students learn how to protect themselves in case of an earthquake, practise leaving the building quietly
7. prepare an "earthquake bag" for their children
8. stories, games, quizzes, surfing the internet, writing reports

---

Lerntipp — So kannst du Reading Skills üben

Sieh dir die Aufgabenstellung vor dem Lesen an und markiere die Schlüsselwörter, nach denen du im Text suchen kannst, um die gefragte Information zu finden. Hier zum Beispiel, Datum/Monatsnamen, **bring, bag, activity**.

Suche dann den Text nach diesen Schlüsselwörtern ab. Nach jedem Schlüsselwort lies den vorherigen und nächsten Satz genau durch, da diese weitere Hinweise enthalten könnten.

Manchmal ist die Information auch anders verpackt, d.h. die Schlüsselwörter aus der Aufgabenstellung tauchen im Text nicht genau so auf (z.B. bei der letzten Frage). Sie sind dann umschrieben, weisen aber auch auf die gewünschte Information hin.

LANGUAGE

1 WORDS A safety team meeting

1 It is important that the students' attitude towards earthquakes changes.
2 The majority of our students have already brought their earthquake bag to school.
3 The earthquake safety exercises mean that the students will know what to do if we experience an earthquake.
4 We need to offer students a realistic experience of an earthquake.
5 Whoever visits our school on ESD should be part of the exercises.
6 After ESD we must meet again and talk about what we need to change next year.
7 We must make sure that all parents know about ESD.
8 We should give parents specific information about the activities on ESD.
9 After ESD every student will know how to act in an earthquake.
10 Whatever happens, I think that ESD will be a success.

2 Getting by in English

1 I get on well with my sister.
2 Don't panic.
3 Things will work out in the end.
4 Can I have a look at the book?
5 What's / What is the hottest country on earth?
6 Some people are still prejudiced / still have prejudices against minorities.

3 GRAMMAR San Jose High School and the ESD

The day before ESD, we were asked to bring our earthquake bags to school. I took my bag to school, and everyone in the class was told to always keep their earthquake bags with them at all times because you never know when there could be an earthquake.
At 9.30 am the school bell rang and the ESD exercises began. Everyone did the exercises: teachers and students. When the bell rang, everybody was told to get on the floor under a table or desk. We waited on the floor for a few minutes until a sign was given. Then we all stood up.
The bell rang again and everyone left the building quietly.
Outside the building all the students were counted. When the head teacher was sure that no one was left in the building, we were told to go back to our classes.

Unit 2 | Lösungen B

Lerntipp Aktiv oder Passiv?

Wenn dir die Unterschiede zwischen Aktiv- und Passivsätzen nicht ganz klar sind, schau dir diese beiden Sätze genau an.

AKTIV	The teachers	counted	all the students.
PASSIV	All the students	were counted.	

Aktivsätze beschreiben, wer oder was etwas tut. (Das Subjekt des Satzes führt die Handlung aus.) Passivsätze beschreiben, mit wem oder womit etwas geschieht. (Wer oder was die Handlung ausführt, ist nicht so wichtig oder gar nicht bekannt oder – wir hier im Beispiel – ganz offensichtlich.)

WRITING

An e-mail to California

Mögliche Lösung:

Dear ... (1P)

Thanks for your e-mail. (1P) It was very interesting to read about your earthquake safety day. (2P) At my school we have a fire exercise twice a year. (1P) The first one is in autumn. Our teachers tell us what we have to do if there is a fire in the school building. (2P) One week later, the fire bell rings and everybody has to leave the building quickly and quietly.

The second exercise is in spring (2P) – the students and the teachers don't know the date, so this is a very good exercise. (2P)

I think it's important that all students take part in this exercise. Fires can be dangerous! (2P)

How was your presentation about Germany? (2P)

Write back soon! (1P)

Love (1P)

...

Lerntipp — Überarbeitung von Lösungen für die **Writing**-Aufgaben

Anhand der folgenden Checkliste kannst du deine Lösung überprüfen und anschließend noch einmal überarbeiten.

- Lies in Zukunft die Musterlösung erst, wenn du deine Lösung mehrere Male überprüft hast.
- Überprüfe, ob du folgende Punkte beachtet hast und hake sie ab.
- Die freien Felder bieten dir Gelegenheit, eigene Punkte einzufügen, auf die du in Zukunft besonders achten willst.

Checkliste

	Datum der Übung								
• Brief/E-Mail: Anrede, Grußformel?									
• Bericht/Geschichte: Überschrift?									
• Alle wichtigen Punkte aus der Aufgabenstellung beachtet?									
• 1–2 einleitende, interessante Sätze am Anfang (ohne Details)?									
• Text mit Absätzen logisch strukturiert?									
• Unterschiedliche Satzstrukturen? (Relativsätze, Sätze mit **linking words**)									
• Abwechslungsreicher Wortschatz (Adjektive, Adverbien, treffende Verben?)									
• Rechtschreibung, Grammatik (Zeiten und Wortstellung) okay?									
• Haben deine Sätze eine sinnvolle Länge (keine „Endlossätze")?									
• Brief/E-Mail: Schlussformel?									
• Bericht/Geschichte: Schlusssatz?									
•									
•									
•									

Unit 3

Lösungen A

LISTENING

🎧 07 Burger day

Good morning, everybody. This is an important announcement from the head teacher.

Today is burger testing day. Get involved and help choose a healthy burger for our school!

Last year we decided that we were going to make our school healthier because we know that our students work harder and get better grades if they eat healthy food. We started by selling fresh fruit at break and now we even sell different types of fruit on different days of the week. We want to keep getting better and hope that we can win the "Healthiest School in Missouri" prize this year.

In our next project we want to make a new, healthy burger, which you, the students, want to eat. A healthy burger? Well, it may sound impossible, but over the past two weeks the students in class 8 have been learning about burgers and have made four delicious, healthy burgers for you to try.

This lunch break I invite you to come to the cafeteria to test the burgers. Here's what you'll be testing:
Burger one is a chicken burger with locally grown tomatoes and lettuce.
Burger two is a beef burger with onions and carrots.
Burger three is a vegetarian burger made with vegetables, nuts and a yoghurt dip.
Burger four is also a beef burger but this one has baked potato chips, tomatoes and salad cream on top.

The burgers come with a healthy, whole-grain roll.

Once you've tried each of the burgers, it's time to choose the one you like best. Class 8 have hung up four posters, one for each burger. You'll get four stickers. If, for example, you only like one of the burgers, then you put all four stickers on that one poster. If you can't decide on one burger you can put the stickers on different posters – it's up to you!

Class 8 and I look forward to seeing you today between 12 and 1. We know you'll enjoy the testing and we can't wait to find out which burger you'll like best.

Help make our school the healthiest school in Missouri!

1 The best poster

Poster of meal 2: Our school wants to win a prize! Join and choose the best burger!

2 About the announcement

1a), 2a), 3c), 4b), 5c), 6b), 7c), 8b)

LANGUAGE

1 WORDS A food mind map

Mögliche Lösungen: Wenn du mehr Wörter gefunden hast als gefordert, zählen diese pro Eintrag 0,5 P extra!

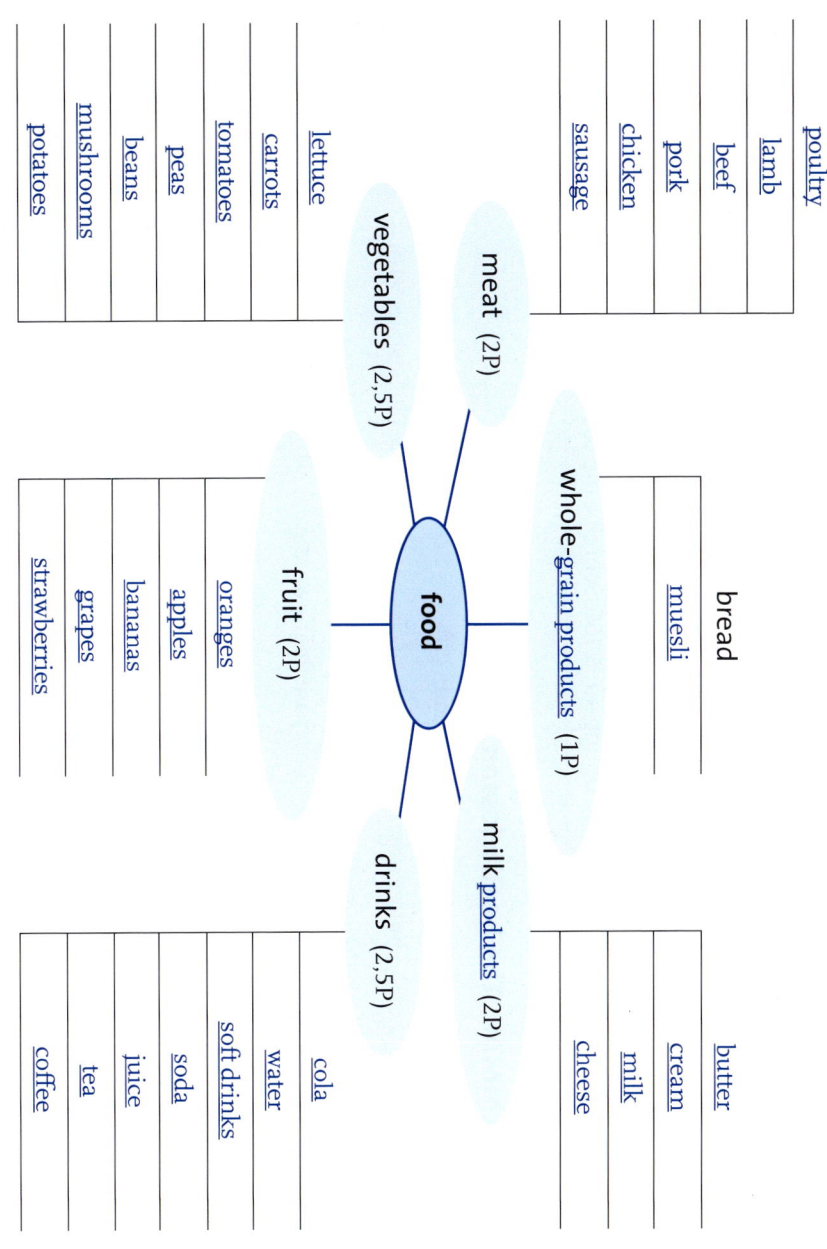

meat (2P): poultry, lamb, beef, pork, chicken, sausage

vegetables (2,5P): lettuce, carrots, tomatoes, peas, beans, mushrooms, potatoes

whole-grain products (1P): bread, muesli

fruit (2P): oranges, apples, bananas, grapes, strawberries

milk products (2P): butter, cream, milk, cheese

drinks (2,5P): cola, water, soft drinks, soda, juice, tea, coffee

2 WORDS We are a healthy school

Das Lösungswort lautet: FRUIT

We believe that a healthy school is a better school. We are sure that **1** healthy kids study better. At our school students get **2** fresh fruit in our **3** cafeteria every day. Our students have also made a healthy burger that **4** contains fewer **5** calories than the **6** average burger. We believe that sport is very important for our students. That's why we make sure that they get daily **7** exercise. They can be **8** active after every second **9** period. We offer lots of different **10** extracurriculars. The school's **11** soccer team is very successful, and lots of the girls are **12** cheerleaders. Come and see our school!

3 GRAMMAR Food words

Countable nouns a/an, one	Uncountable nouns some
egg	milk
tomato	water
whole-grain product	cheese
apple	tea
lemon	meat

Unit 3 | Lösungen A

4 GRAMMAR Our healthy meals

1. Meal 1 is a healthy burger with some lettuce, two tomatoes and an apple. (2P)
2. Meal 2 is some fish, some cheese, two carrots and a fruit salad. (2P)
3. Meal 3 is a sausage, some beans, some vegetables and some strawberries. (2P)

Lerntipp Zählbare und nicht zählbare Nomen

Nicht zählbare Nomen stehen nie im Plural. Das ist manchmal anders als im Deutschen, z. B. bei some **homework, information** und **news**. Präge dir diese Ausnahmen besonders ein.
Lies noch mal die Übung in deinem Englischbuch auf S. 64 und das Grammar-File 3 auf S. 165 nach und mache anschließend die Can you …?-Übung auf S. 166. Schreibe die Lösungen in dein Lernheft.

5 GRAMMAR The health lesson

1. We know that young people often eat fast food. (1P)
2. We are proud that the burgers that the students of class 8 made are really healthy. (1P)
3. Lots of people work so much that they aren't able to cook. (0,5P)
4. Then they often eat fast food and don't prepare their own meals. (0,5P)
5. Many people say that the burgers sold in fast food restaurants are a quick and cheap lunch. (0,5P)
6. I don't like burgers. My favourite dish is the spaghetti that my sister often makes. (0,5P)

6 GRAMMAR Our burger project

After we had found a lot of information on the internet, we talked about it. When we had discussed the healthy burgers for more than an hour, we decided it was time to try and make some. After we had written the shopping list we went to the supermarket. In the lunch break we tried the different burgers which we had prepared in the school's kitchen. They were all delicious.

Now you

Mögliche Lösung:

1. After I had done my homework, I went to the swimming-pool.
2. I didn't watch the film after my friend had told me the plot.
3. After I had told her about my good mark in English, my mum was very happy.

Lerntipp Simple past oder past perfect?

Lies noch mal das Grammar-File 5 auf S. 167 nach und mache anschließend die Can you …?-Übung. Schreibe die Lösungen in dein Lernheft.

MEDIATION

1 A health project

Wenn du noch mehr Mediation üben möchtest, schau dir die Übung auf S. 50 an.

a) Man wird seltener krank, kann besser lernen (2P)

b) **Hauptidee 1**: Obst zu den Schulmahlzeiten hinzufügen, z.B. Obststücke in den Salat hinein tun, auf Obst der Jahreszeit achten, Bratäpfel oder Erdbeeren zum Nachtisch (3P)
Hauptidee 2: Wenn Essen gut aussieht, regt es den Appetit an, z.B. Obst mit unterschiedlichen Farben, Frucht-Smoothies mit Milch oder Joghurt, klein geschnittenes, nett hergerichtetes Obst (3P)
Hauptidee 3: Ideen für Zwischenmahlzeiten, z.B. klein geschnittenes, frisches Obst, Trockenfrüchte (3P)

c) Obst (auch Melonen oder Orangen) vor dem Essen abwaschen und abtrocknen (2P)

STUDY SKILLS

Writing a summary

Mögliche Lösung:

The story is about a school project called burger testing day. (2P) The school wants to make its own healthy "school burger", because it wants its students to become healthier and it wants to become the healthiest school in Missouri. (4P)

Class 8 has made different healthy burgers. (2P) They would like the other students to test the burgers. (2P) Three girls take part in the testing. First they look at the burgers and guess which one they will like best. Then the girls try the burgers and each one of them chooses the burger or burgers which they like best. (4P) One girl chooses burger number four, her friends choose two different burgers each and in the end number four becomes the school burger. (3P)

The school organizes other healthy food projects. The girls eat more healthily and at the end of the year they all get better grades! (3P)

Unit 3 Lösungen B

READING

A letter from Hermann

1 About the letter

167 Wine Street
Hermann
65041 MO
USA
March 25

Dear Sir or Madam,

I'm a student in grade 9 at Hermann High School, Missouri, USA. I'm 15 years old and I'm interested in doing an exchange with a school in Germany next year. I thought you might be able to help me. Maybe there's a student at your school who is interested in taking part in an exchange and would like to come to Hermann.

I live together with my mom and dad and my two little sisters, Anna and Lucy. They're five and eight years old. My parents have a hotel in Hermann, and we have a lot of German speaking guests. I'd like to be better at German so that I can talk more with the guests and help my parents with German e-mails and letters. At school my favorite subjects are Science and Math. In my free time I like cooking for my family and friends – I make a great lasagne! I also play baseball in the school team. Here at my school we have a German club, which I joined two years ago. I can understand easy German conversations quite well. Coming to Germany would mean that I could learn lots more German and find out more about German people.

I'm looking for an exchange partner who is about my age. He/She doesn't have to have the same hobbies as me, but what's important is that we are both open to new experiences! I'm interested in the history of Germany and would love to visit Berlin while I'm on the exchange. It would be good if my partner was interested in going there as well. I'd like to come to Germany from September to February and I thought that my exchange partner could come to Hermann from March to August. Of course, we can talk more about the dates later on.

I hope I have the chance to come to Bad Arolsen next school year, and my family and I are really looking forward to welcoming a German student to Hermann. Thank you for your help.

Yours,
Jason Winter

2 A notice for the school's notice board

2 • parents have a hotel in Hermann
 • two sisters (Anna and Lucy) five and eight years old (2P)

3 • in grade 9
 • Science and Math (2P)

4 has been in a German club for two years, understands easy conversations (2P)

5 plays baseball in school team, likes cooking for family and friends (makes a great lasagne) (2P)

6 wants to be better at German to help parents in hotel, wants to get to know Germany, interested in German history (3P)

7 Jason in Germany: September–February, German partner in Hermann: March–August, but dates can be decided later (3P)

8 Jason Winter, 167 Wine Street, Hermann, 65041 MO, USA (1P)

LANGUAGE

1 WORDS The Winters are discussing the exchange

Mr Winter Well Jason, let's talk about your idea of doing an exchange. The German school <u>system</u> is different to ours, so you might have some difficulties when you come back. You'll have different <u>classes</u> to your classes here in Hermann. I think you'll have to <u>study</u> a lot more than you're doing at the moment to keep your <u>grades</u>.

Jason You're probably right, Dad. But staying in Germany will be really good for me. My German will be excellent, I'll know a lot about German <u>traditions</u>, which will help us with the hotel when we have <u>foreign</u> guests who speak German.

Mrs Winter I think we need to talk about the German exchange partner. Where could we find a nice boy? What about Hermann's <u>sister city</u> Bad Arolsen?

Jason Good idea, Mom. But I can write to other schools too. They can put a notice up on the school's <u>bulletin board</u>. I'm sure there'll be students who want <u>to get involved in</u> an exchange.

2 GRAMMAR At my German school

When I lived in Stuttgart, school played an important part in my daily life. (0,5P) I really liked <u>the</u> school I went to. (0,5P) Usually in Germany lessons start very early in the morning but <u>the</u> lessons at my school didn't start before 8.30. (1,5P) Lucky me! History was my favorite class. (0,5P) I'm interested in history, especially in <u>the</u> history of Germany after the Second World War. (1P) I didn't really miss much about <u>the</u> US while I was there. (0,5P) But one thing I did miss was <u>the</u> extracurricular sports activities at school. (0,5P) The Germans like sport, but they don't have school teams. (0,5P) If you want to play sport, you have to join a club. (0,5P) If you like soccer you can watch matches every Saturday afternoon. (0,5P) I often went to watch VFB Stuttgart, <u>the</u> local team, play. (0,5P)

3 GRAMMAR Thoughts and questions about the exchange

1 I want to have as <u>much</u> information as possible before I decide.
2 How <u>many</u> students can go on the exchange to Germany this year?
3 How <u>much</u> money will I need?
4 Will we have to do <u>much</u> work to prepare for the exchange?
5 I found <u>many</u> interesting articles written by exchange students on the internet.

Unit 3 | Lösungen B

WRITING

A letter to Hermann

Mögliche Lösung:

Leon Schießer
Traubenweg 4
34454 Bad Arolsen
March 17 (2P)

Dear Jason, (1P)

My teacher showed me the letter you wrote about the exchange. I like the idea of going to Hermann – so here's my letter to you. I'm 14 years old, but I'll be 15 soon. We – that's my dad, my mum and my sister Lara (she's 12) live in a small house in Bad Arolsen. (2P)
My hobbies are football and swimming. I've never played baseball, but there's a baseball club in the next city. (2P)
My favourite subjects are English and French and we both like German history. (2P) I hope we can visit Berlin together. (2P)
The school year here starts in August, so maybe you could come here then. Do you think you could stay until January? (2P) Then I could come to Hermann in February and stay until July. (2P)
Write back soon – I'm looking forward to hearing from you. (2P)

Yours,
Leon (1P)

Lerntipp Briefe schreiben

Mehr Tipps zum Schreiben eines Briefes findest du in deinem Englischbuch auf S. 62 und im Skills File auf S. 156.

SPEAKING

🔊 08 Calling your exchange partner

Mike Hello, how are you?

Moritz Fine thanks. I'm counting the days until you come to Germany.

Mike Me too, I can't wait! I'm calling because I've got some questions for you.

Moritz OK.

Mike Well, let's start with the clothes. What will I need to bring? What about the temperature in winter? Is there anything important that I shouldn't forget?

Moritz You'll need stuff like trousers, T-shirts and pullovers of course. You should bring some warm clothes for the winter. It can get cold here, you know, sometimes the temperature is minus 10 degrees. So don't forget some warm boots.

Mike What about school? What clothes should I bring for school?

Moritz You won't need anything special for school, just your everyday clothes. We don't have a school uniform.

Mike OK. What about the school times? When do classes start in the morning?

Moritz School starts quite early, at 7.30.

Mike And what about the afternoon? Are there lessons then too? And is there a school cafeteria where we can have lunch?

Moritz There are lessons in the afternoon on Mondays, Tuesdays and Thursdays. There's a new cafeteria at school where we can have lunch. There are two meals to choose from every day.

Mike Awesome! And when do you usually get home in the afternoon?

Moritz If there are lessons in the afternoon, I usually get home at about 4.30 and on the other days I get home by 1.30.

Mike You know what Moritz, I'd love to go to Berlin. How far away is it from where you live and how could we get there?

Moritz Berlin is quite far away, I think it's about 350 kilometres. The train takes about four hours. We can stay in a youth hostel, that's not too expensive.

Mike Great, I hope we can do that. Now – one more question. Maybe it's a difficult one. I'd like to bring a little present for the head teacher of your school because I want to thank him for his help. Can you give me a tip? Any idea what he likes?

Moritz Oh, he loves books. Why don't you bring him a book about Hermann. I'm sure he'd like that.

Mike Good idea, thanks. Right, that's all for today, we can phone again next week.

Moritz OK, bye for now, speak to you next week.

Unit 3 | Lösungen B

🎧 09 Now you

Lerntipp	Sprechen üben

1. Wenn dir die Antworten zunächst schwerfallen, bearbeite diese Übung nicht auf einmal, sondern in Abschnitten.
2. Nimm deine Antworten auf!
3. Vergleiche deine Antwort mit der Musterlösung.
4. Kannst du noch ausführlicher antworten? Dann wiederhole die Übung oder den Abschnitt.

Mögliche Lösung:

Jason Hello, how are you?
You Fine thanks. And you? (2P)
Jason I'm well, I'm counting the days until I come to Germany. Now listen, I've got some questions for you.
You OK. (1P)
Jason Well, let's start with the clothes. What will I need to bring? What about the temperature in winter? Is there anything important that I shouldn't forget?
You You'll need trousers, T-shirts and pullovers of course. And something warm for the winter. Don't forget warm boots and a warm jacket. It can get cold here in winter. Sometimes the temperature is minus 12 degrees. (3P)
Jason What about school? What clothes should I bring for school?
You We don't have a school uniform, so you'll only need your everyday clothes for school. (2P)
Jason OK. What about the school times? When do classes start in the morning?
You School starts quite early. The first lesson is at 7.50. (1P)
Jason Hm, and what about the afternoon? Are there lessons then too? And is there a school cafeteria where we can have lunch?
You There are lessons in the afternoon on Mondays and Wednesdays. There are no afternoon lessons on the other days. We can have lunch at the cafeteria. (3P)
Jason Awesome! And when do you usually get home in the afternoon?
You On days without afternoon lessons I get home at about 2.00 and on the other days I get home by 4.45. (2P)
Jason You know that I'd love to go to Berlin. How far away is it from your town and how could we get there?
You Berlin isn't far, about 250 kilometres. The train takes about two hours. (2P)
Jason Great, I hope we can do that. Now – just one more question. Maybe it's a difficult one. I'd like to bring a little present for the head teacher of your school because I want to thank him for his help. Can you give me a tip? Any idea what he likes?
You Oh, that's really difficult. What about a T-shirt from Hermann? (2P)
Jason Good idea, thanks. Right, that's all for today, we can phone again next week.
You OK, bye for now, speak to you next week. (2P)

MEDIATION

A day trip to Heidelberg

10 a)

Your teacher Wir treffen uns hier vor der Schule, der Bus fährt um Punkt 7 Uhr ab. Da wir mindestens zwei Stunden bis Heidelberg benötigen, können wir nicht warten, falls sich jemand verspätet. Also, bitte unbedingt den Wecker stellen.

Student I didn't get all the details about tomorrow. Do we have to bring an alarm clock?

You No, you don't need to bring an alarm clock. But it's important that you arrive at the school on time. The bus leaves at 7 o'clock. (3P)

11 b)

Your teacher Wir werden etwa um 10:30 Uhr in Heidelberg eintreffen. Das hängt natürlich vom Verkehr auf der Autobahn ab. Unser erster Programmpunkt ist dann die Besichtigung des Schlosses. Vergesst euren Fotoapparat nicht. Es gibt viele schöne Motive. Vor dem Schloss werden wir auch ein Gruppenfoto machen. Gegen 11:30 gehen wir dann in die Innenstadt, wo wir an einer Stadtführung teilnehmen. Die dauert etwa eine Dreiviertelstunde. Die Informationen, die ihr auf dieser Führung bekommt, sollten übrigens in euren Bericht über diese Exkursion einfließen. Also haltet bitte Papier und Schreibzeug bereit!

Student I understood that we're going to visit Heidelberg Castle. That's great. But what was that about the camera? And do we have to write something?

You We should bring our cameras because there are lots of interesting things to take photos of. Also we're going to take a photo of the whole class in front of the castle. (2P) We need a pen and some paper for our tour of Heidelberg. We have to write a report later. (2P)

Your teacher Ja und dann beginnt eure Freizeit in Heidelberg. Ihr dürft euch Heidelberg dann noch genauer ansehen, in Gruppen mit mindestens drei Personen. Die Personen einer Gruppe schreiben ihre Namen auf meine Liste hier, damit ich weiß, wer mit wem unterwegs ist. Natürlich könnt ihr auch einkaufen gehen – ganz wie ihr wollt. Nur bitte ich euch, wieder pünktlich zum Treffpunkt zu kommen. Wir treffen uns um 15:30 Uhr bei unserem Bus.

Student What was that about three people? I didn't understand what the teacher said.

You In the afternoon we have free time in Heidelberg. We have to be in groups of at least three people. We have to write our names on the teacher's list. (2P)

Student And do we have to do anything special in our groups?

You No, we can do what we like. (1P)

Student And where do we meet after that?

You We meet at 3.30 pm at the coach. (1P)

Your teacher Wir werden dann gegen 18 Uhr zurück sein. Der Busfahrer lässt uns am Bahnhof aussteigen, so dass ihr von dort aus nach Hause gehen könnt. Also, ich hoffe, wir werden einen schönen gemeinsamen Tag haben. Eine Sache noch, Herrschaften! Nehmt euch auf jeden Fall genügend zu essen und zu trinken für den ganzen Tag mit und denkt an eine Mütze oder einen Hut gegen die Sonne. Es wird heiß!

Student We'll be back by 6 pm. Is there anything else that's important for me to know?

You Yes, be sure to bring drinks, some food and a hat or a cap. (3P)

Unit 4 — Lösungen A

LISTENING

🎧 12 CASA – Come and see Atlanta!

There's no better way to see the sights of Atlanta than with a C-A-S-A-tour. C-A-S-A – that's short for "Come and see Atlanta"!

Atlanta, the largest city in the south-east, is a must for your stay in Georgia. We have many years of experience showing people around: we've been taking visitors on trips around Atlanta for 15 years! Our experience is your advantage: no matter if you're travelling alone, with your family or in a large group, if you're here for business or on holiday – we have the right tour for you.

CASA offers all kinds of tours from quick two hour visits to a half or even a full day tour – anything is possible. We're ready to listen to your wishes. On the two hour tour you'll see the most important sights here in Atlanta. If you book a full day you can choose from many different attractions.

Our friendly CASA guides will show you the most important places in Atlanta and give you all the facts you need. They'll tell you stories about the history of Atlanta, the people who have lived here and, of course, they're ready to answer your questions – no matter what they're about. And – we have French and Spanish speaking guides too.

If you're interested in history, the City of Atlanta invites you to explore the city's past. Take the History Tour and visit all the important historical sights – even the famous King Center!

On our Tour 21 you'll visit CNN and the "World of Coca-Cola", you will be shown downtown Atlanta and "Underground Atlanta", a large area below street level with many shops and restaurants. We have information about six other tours on our website.

If you have any special wishes or ideas – talk to us. You tell us your special wishes and how much time you've got for the tour – and we'll work out a personalized tour for you or your group! By the way, it's no problem if there are just two or three of you. We'll organize a tour for you in one of our comfortable cars.

And last but not least: we offer a pick up service from your hotel; just let us know where you're staying. One of our drivers will come and meet you. After the tour he'll drop you off back at the hotel.

CASA – Come and see Atlanta – your address in the capital of Georgia! Phone today or come and see us at one of our offices in Atlanta.

About CASA

1a), 2b), 3c), 4b), 5c), 6b)

LANGUAGE

1 WORDS Martin Luther King

1. Don't miss the chance to visit the King Center <u>during</u> your visit to Atlanta.
2. The young Martin Luther King worked for a Baptist church as a <u>minister</u>.
3. At that time blacks didn't have the same rights as whites – there was <u>segregation</u>.
4. Martin Luther King fought for <u>civil rights</u> for black people.
5. At that time African Americans and white American were kept <u>apart</u>.
6. In 1963 Martin Luther King became famous through the <u>March</u> on Washington.
7. There he made his famous <u>speech</u>.
8. April 4th is the <u>anniversary</u> of his death.
9. Most people who go to the King Center are very <u>impressed</u>.

2 GRAMMAR A weekend in Atlanta

a)
1. John has already visited the official Atlanta website.
2. Tim and Sue have already searched for tours of Atlanta.
3. Tim hasn't bought a map yet.
4. Sue and Sally haven't found out about train times yet.
5. Sally has already looked for cheap hotels.
6. Sally hasn't phoned a hotel yet.

b)
Mögliche Lösungen:
1. I've already talked to my trainer about the match next weekend.
2. I've already asked my parents about the party on Saturday.
3. I haven't read Susan's book yet.
4. I haven't spoken to my parents about my mark in Chemistry yet.

Lerntipp Zeitenbildung

Wiederhole nochmals die Zeiten mithilfe der Tabelle auf S. 4 in diesem Lösungsheft. Setze **I am, he writes, we don't ask** in die entsprechenden Zeitformen. (Lösungen s. S. 38)

3 GRAMMAR At the CASA office

1. The office has been full of customers since we opened this morning.
2. The other tour guides and I have worked without a break since 8 o'clock this morning.
3. Visitors have called about more than twelve tours since Monday.
4. I've talked to three visitors for more than 30 minutes.
5. I haven't had time to read my e-mails for 24 hours.

Lerntipp Since und for

Merke dir jeweils ein Beispiel: **since** the year 2008, **for** three years. Präge dir folgende Eselsbrücke ein: **since** bei Zeit**punkt**, **for** bei Zeitraum. Bearbeite dann die Can you?-Aufgabe auf S. 163 oben in deinem Englischbuch.

Unit 4 | Lösungen A

Lösungen zu S. 37:

simple present: I am, he writes, we don't ask
simple past: I was, he wrote, we didn't ask
present perfect: I have been, he has written, we haven't asked
will-future: I will be, he will write, we will ask
present progressive: I am being, he is writing, we aren't asking
past progressive: I was being, he was writing, we weren't asking

MEDIATION

At the CASA travel agency

Mögliche Lösung:

Frau Kurz	Sagst du bitte der Dame, dass wir eine Tour für vier Personen mitmachen möchten.
Niklas	Hello. We'd like to go on a tour of Atlanta. There are four of us. (1P)
Lady	Let's see. We've got different tours to choose from. What exactly do you want to see?
Niklas	Sie haben unterschiedliche Touren. Sie fragt, was wir genau sehen wollen. (2P)
Herr Kurz	Na ja, auf jeden Fall die Innenstadt, finde ich.
Niklas	Well, we'd definitely like to see downtown Atlanta. (1P)
Lady	Then I can offer you our Tour 21. You'll see all the sights in downtown Atlanta, you'll visit CNN and the World of Coca-Cola and the tour ends at Underground Atlanta.
Niklas	Sie bietet uns die Tour 21 an. Das ist eine Tour, auf der man alle Sehenswürdigkeiten der Innenstadt besichtigt, man kann CNN und die World of Coca-Cola ansehen und die Tour endet dann in Underground Atlanta. (4P)
Frau Kurz	Was ist denn Underground Atlanta?
Niklas	Could you please explain what "Underground Atlanta" is? (1P)
Lady	It's a large area below street level with many shops, restaurants and cinemas. It's an ideal place to relax after the long day tour. You could also have dinner there.
Niklas	Sie sagt, dass es ein großes Gelände unter der Erde ist mit vielen Läden, Restaurants und Kinos. Sie meint auch, es sei ideal, um nach der langen Tagestour zu entspannen. Außerdem könnten wir dort auch zu Abend essen. (4P)
Herr Kurz	Mir gefällt die Tour. Niklas, frag bitte noch, wo und wann die Tour beginnt.
Niklas	My father thinks the tour sounds interesting. Where and when does it start? (2P)
Lady	If you're staying in a hotel in Atlanta, we can pick you up there at 10.30 in the morning.
Niklas	Sie sagt, wenn wir in einem Hotel hier in Atlanta wohnen, holen sie uns dort um 10:30 morgens ab. (2P)
Frau Kurz	Das ist ja wunderbar. Frag bitte, wieviel es für vier Personen kostet.
Niklas	How much is the tour for four people, please? (1P)
Lady	We have a special offer for families: it's $42 for the four of you.
Niklas	Sie haben ein Sonderangebot für Familien. Das Familienticket kostet $ 42 für uns alle. (1P)
Herr Kurz	Dann buchen wir die Tour für morgen.
Niklas	OK, we'd like to go on this tour tomorrow, please. (1P)

Lösungen B

Unit 4

READING

About the web discussion

1 April, USA (2P)
2 visit parents at work, activities, workshops (3P)
3 at an office (1P)
4 interview people, meet bosses, games (word search, puzzles) (3P)
5 meetings, lunch with dad in cafeteria, take messages, make photocopies (drei davon) (3P)
6 Are children old enough? Are there activities/workshops? Don't miss lessons? Is child interested? (drei davon) (3P)

LANGUAGE

1 WORDS TYCTWD at CNN

a)

Time	2.00 pm	2.30 pm	3.00 pm	3.30 pm	4.00 pm	4.30 pm	5.00 pm
Title	Love your pets	Georgia's best school team: finals	Big brother	The price is right	True blood	Georgia news	CSI Miami
Programme	documentary	competition	reality show	game show	*drama series*	news	crime series

b)

(to) be on, to watch, to last (for), TV listings, prime time, comedy series, newsreader, viewer (*vier davon*)

c)

Mögliche Lösungen:

My favourite programme is on at 5 pm.
The following programme lasts 45 minutes.
I love watching game shows.

2 WORDS Jenny at her mum's office

Last week Jenny and her mum went to work together. It was TYCTWD. Jenny's mum is a journalist. Jenny was very impressed when she saw the big building her mum works in. As soon as they opened the door of her mum's office, she immediately started the computer. Her mum told her to look for some pictures for her next article. So Jenny entered some key words in the search engine of a picture database. TYCTWD was a valuable experience for Jenny. Jenny liked the work so much that she wished the day would last forever. Jenny was disappointed that she couldn't join her mum the next day too.

Unit 4 | Lösungen B

3 GRAMMAR TYCTWD at AUM Technology

1 They have offered TYCTWD for more than ten years now.
2 At the start only a few kids visited the company. But since 2002 this has changed. In that year the company started to offer special activities for the kids.
3 For the last five years the working parents have always prepared something special.
4 Since 2010 they have even asked some newspaper reporters to come and report on the event.

4 GRAMMAR This year's TYCTWD

1 At 7 o'clock the cleaners prepared the room where the kids were welcomed.
2 Mrs Sutterland was very nice and made some muffins.
3 13 children were invited to take part in TYCTWD.
4 The kids waited in the lobby for the boss.
5 Then they were welcomed in the cafeteria.
6 This year's TYCTWD began with an orange juice for everybody.

Lerntipp Schwierigkeiten bei Aktiv oder Passiv?

Arbeite noch einmal das Grammar File 2 auf S. 157 in deinem Englischbuch durch. Wiederhole dann den Lerntipp aus Unit 2, S. 24 in diesem Lösungsheft.

WRITING

1 Your opinion of TYCTWD

Mögliche Lösung:

Hi, I'm 14 and I'm from Germany. (2P)

The students at my school sometimes spend some weeks doing work experience in companies in Dresden. But we do this work experience on our own, not together with our parents. Some companies take part in Girls' and Boys' Days too. (3P)

I think the American TYCTWD is a brilliant idea. I would love to have something like that here. (2P)

It's a good way to find out about your parents' jobs and it helps you with school too. (4P)

Here's another idea for an activity: students could take pictures and write a report about their TYCTWD. (3P)

I wish everyone good luck. (1P)

Tom | 14 | Dresden | Germany

SPEAKING

🎧 13 Eric's day at the restaurant

Hello, everybody. I want to tell you about my Take Your Child To Work Day. I spent the day together with my father who is a cook at a French Restaurant here in Atlanta.
Well, our day started early. I had to get up at 5.30 in the morning. After breakfast Dad and I went shopping. We had to get fresh meat, fish and vegetables. We went to the market where we were almost the first customers. That was really good, because we could pick out the best things.
When we arrived at the restaurant, it was about 9.30 – time for a meeting with the other people who work in the kitchen. Dad told them about the jobs that had to be done that day. After a short coffee break we started preparing the salad. At about 12.30 the dessert was prepared. During the lunch break I was able to talk to most of the people who work at the restaurant. It was interesting to find out about their different jobs.
In the afternoon we carried on with the dessert. And after that we started preparing the vegetables. I also helped with the tables. Later everybody worked on the meat and the fish. At the end of the day I tried the delicious meal that I had helped to prepare. My dad's day wasn't finished till 10.45 pm.
I enjoyed my day at the restaurant because now I know how much my dad works! I also understand why he loves his job so much. But I don't think I want to become a cook.

Now you

Mögliche Lösung:

Hello, my name is Maria. Last week it was Girls' Day and I went to a garage. I wanted to find out more about what a car mechanic does. (2P)
I arrived at 8 am and stayed at the garage until 5 pm. (2P) Of course, I was the only girl there and I felt a bit lonely at the beginning. But one of the mechanics was very nice and showed me around.
The garage is very busy and lots of men work there. They were working on eight cars when I was there. There weren't so many things for me to do, but I helped to clean one of the cars and after that I went to the post office to get a parcel. (8P)
I liked the atmosphere at the garage, everybody was very friendly and they all seemed to be happy. I think that girls can be good car mechanics too if they like cars and don't mind having dirty hands in the evening. It was a really great experience. (4P)

Kompetenztest

TEIL 1: LISTENING

Radio and TV in your lives

🎧 14

Larry Hello everybody, this is Larry from Radio Today. You're listening to Teatime, your afternoon programme from four till six with all your favourite music. Yesterday we asked you to tell us what time of the day you listen to the radio, when you watch TV and about the programmes you like best. People from all parts of Britain have called us. Thank you so much. Now today we want to listen to some of the calls we got on our answering machine. So let's start right away.

Emily Good afternoon, this is Emily from Exeter. Well, I couldn't live without radio. It's the radio that wakes me up in the morning at 6.30. I love to hear some good music in the morning. I keep listening to it until I leave the house to go to school at 7.45. I'm a teacher you know. So of course I don't listen to the radio during the day, not until I come home after school at around 5 o'clock. Then I enjoy listening to your programme Teatime. Then I keep listening to the radio, I always need some music around. I don't watch much TV, but I try to watch the evening news most nights, you know – just so I know what's going on in the world. Bye-bye.

Steve Hi, I'm Steve from Canterbury. My day starts with TV. When I'm having breakfast at 8 o'clock I always watch the morning show. I like watching something fun and getting information at the same time. So, no radio in the morning but I listen to the radio all day while I'm working at my shop. I sell clothes for young people, so music is important for the people shopping too. I think it makes people happy when they hear a song they really like on the radio. As soon as I come home after work, I turn on the TV and I don't turn it off until I go to bed. I don't really have any favourite programmes, I think TV is just a good way to relax after a long day at work. Bye.

Anne Hi, I'm Anne. Well, I don't like listening to the radio or watching TV in the morning – in fact I love having a quiet morning without any media. But I always listen to the radio when I'm in my car during the day. Time seems to run more quickly when you're listening to some good music and to programmes like Teatime. Of course, I love watching TV after dinner together with my husband. We usually watch a nice film, or we watch the football. My husband is mad about football, you know. Okay – bye.

	In the morning			During the day			In the evening		
	Radio	TV	Nothing	Radio	TV		Radio	TV	
Emily	✓			✓ When? _in the afternoon_			What? _music_	✓ What? _news_	
Steve		✓		✓ When? _all day_			What?	✓ What? _anything_	
Anne			✓	✓ When? _in the car_			What?	✓ What? _films, football_	

TEIL 2: SPEAKING
Me, my day, radio and TV

Mögliche Lösung:

Hello, my name is Lisa, I'm a German student and I'm on holiday in Southampton at the moment. I'd like to tell you about my day in Germany.

I get up at 6.30 am. That's when I start listening to the radio, and of course I listen to music. I carry on listening to my favourite programme while I'm in the bathroom. Then I have breakfast and go to school. Of course I can't listen to the radio at school. When I come home after school, I have lunch and then I do my homework. Of course with music! I think I finish my homework quicker when I listen to my favourite music. When I've finished my homework, I watch some TV. I like watching soap operas, and I try not to miss a single episode of my favourite soap, GZSZ.

In the evenings I sometimes watch TV, but not every evening. I play football and tennis myself, so I mostly watch sports programmes. When the tennis at Wimbledon is on TV, I watch all the matches.

TEIL 3: MEDIATION

1 Ist es eine geführte Tour? Und was können wir bei der Führung alles sehen? *(3 Dinge)* (4P)
   Ja, die Tour ist geführt. Wir bekommen einen Einblick in viele Sendungen, die bei Southwest Radio and TV gemacht werden. Wir sehen ein Fernsehstudio und Radiostudios und hören, wie Radiosendungen gemacht werden. (4P)

2 Kann man da auch selbst etwas machen und wenn ja, was? *(2 Dinge)* (2P)
   Ja, es gibt ein interaktives Studio, in dem wir selbst die Wettervorhersage präsentieren und selbst bei einem Radiohörspiel mitmachen können, komplett mit Soundeffekten. (1P)

3 Wie lange dauert die Tour?
   Eine Stunde und 45 Minuten. (1P)

4 Um wie viel Uhr beginnen die Touren?
   Es gibt zwei Touren, um 10 Uhr und um 15:15 Uhr. Sie finden dienstags statt und ab 14. Juli auch mittwochs und samstags. (2P)

5 Wie ist es mit der Gruppengröße?
   Es dürfen maximal 25 Teilnehmer pro Tour mitgehen. (1P)

6 Gibt es sonst Dinge, die wir als Schulklasse beachten müssen?
   Man muss mindestens 10 Jahre alt sein. Wenn Schüler und Schülerinnen unter 16 an der Tour teilnehmen, müssen sie von zwei Erwachsenen begleitet werden. (2P)

7 Darf man überall fotografieren und auch Videos drehen?
   Man darf fotografieren, wenn es uns von dem Tour Guide erlaubt wird. Videos dürfen nur in dem interaktiven Studio gedreht werden. (2P)

8 Muss man sich da anmelden und wie viel kostet der Besuch?
   Ja, man muss vorbuchen. Der Besuch kostet aber nichts / ist umsonst/kostenlos. (2P)

Kompetenztest 43

Kompetenztest

TEIL 4: READING

2 What are the most famous soaps on British TV? Coronation Street, EastEnders
3 Where do the characters in these soap operas live? Manchester, East End of London
4 What are these soaps about? Everyday family life, problems, comedy
5 Who watched the soaps when they first started? Housewives
6 What is the name of the first ever British soap? Can you watch it on television?
   The Archers, made for radio
7 What did companies selling washing powder have to do with soap operas?
   produced/supported soaps, viewers bought products

TEIL 5: WORDS

a)
1 ... the different sections of a soap opera shown three, four or five times a week: episodes
2 ... people who act in films, theatre or television: actors
3 ... people who watch TV: viewers
4 ... (to) make someone sad or angry: (to) upset someone

b)
1 many: a few
2 different: the same
3 serious: funny
4 daytime: nighttime

c)
2 produce, sell, buy, watch
3 product, pub, company, shop
4 channel, film, programme, newspaper
5 soap, support, water, shower

TEIL 6: WRITING

Mögliche Lösung:

My favourite film (1P)

My favourite film is Avatar. (1P) It is about a moon called Pandora where the Na'vi people live. We had to wear funny glasses because it was in 3D. (2P)

I saw Avatar at the big cinema in town with a group of my friends on a Saturday afternoon. (3P)

The main character Jake Sully is played by Sam Worthington. (2P) He becomes an avatar so that he looks like one of the Na'vi and can find out more about them. (3P)

The main reason I liked Avatar was because of the new world they created. It was really beautiful and so real. The fight scenes were great in 3D too! (3P)